315 *Madison av. Albany N. Y.*

From Melvil Dewey to some personal friends

Soon after the American library association and Library journal were started in 1876, seeing the need of long continued and hard work on the part of those giving their lives to important undertakings, I became convinced that one of the greatest problems in our new field was to find a way to get most health and strength for the coming year's work from the summer outing, which seldom gave wholly satisfactory results for time and money spent. This problem confronts every one who wishes to accomplish the greatest practical results in any field.

Mrs Dewey and I believe that we have found a solution in the club started by us in 1895, the permanence of which is now assured, as its last is by far its most successful season. We have studied the question from the first, not as a summer diversion, but as one of the most serious of modern life, deserving our best thought and effort, believing that as great a service can be rendered to the public in this way as by founding a new library or school.

We take great pride in what is already accomplished and wish our personal friends to know more of it, and are therefore sending with this letter the club handbook to those who we

Lake library, canoe and boathouses and lakeside dining rooms

Lake Placid Club

Organized 1895

Morningside   Moose Island

Adirondack Lodge

' Heart of the Adirondacks '

HANDBOOK

MORNINGSIDE N. Y.

1901

Spelling

Simplified spellings used are recommended by the English philological society and the American philological association including the leading language scholars of Oxford, Cambridge and the American universities, also by the latest and most authoritativ dictionaries The full list is in the body of the *Standard*, appended to the *Century* and prefixt to Webster

CONTENTS

Clubhouse 1899

Circular

The Lake Placid Club is not open to the public, but has ample accommodations for more than its present membership, and to keep cooperativ cost at the limit fixt, wishes all its rooms occupied as fast as it finds thuroly congenial people. It increases its numbers only on personal invitations by members to those who would add to the attractions of the club home at Morningside. This circular is to send as a suggestion for the summer to such friends, who if interested can get fuller information described on p. 20.

Object. Cooperation among congenial people secures the privileges of an ideal summer home in ideal surroundings. It is organized and administerd solely to give the greatest possible new health and strength for the coming year for time and money spent to secure 7 things: health, comfort and convenience, quiet and rest, congenial companionship, attractiv recreations, beautiful natural surroundings, and as moderate living expenses as is consistent with high standards in each of the above chief aims. For the unusual advantages secured by 7 years of earnest, skilful, conscientious work and liberal expenditure see these heads in the Handbook.

Not a hotel. The club is a cooperativ summer home of a large number of congenial people. Having no transient guests, it differs as much from the atmosphere, spirit and management of a hotel as a refined private home differs from a conventional boarding house. The table and houses are in charge of acknowledged experts in domestic science who have a fixt salary

---

Spelling. Simplified spellings used are recommended by the English philological society and the American philologcial association including the leading language scholars of Oxford, Cambridge and the American univerxities, also by the latest and most authoritativ dictionaries, which give the full list in the body of the *Standard*, appended to the *Century* and prefixt to Webster.

North end of Morningside from Westwood

with no direct interest in receipts. The club plans are shaped
by prominent workers in the new science of home economics,
who hold their annual conferences at the club. A leading purpose is to show practically that the most attractiv home and
table may also in the highest degree illustrate the teaching of
modern science as to health and home comforts. It is no place
for display. It believes in early hours, informality and simplicity.
It hopes to be proof against all inroads of mere fashion.

Forest

Distinctiv features.
The club has clearly
defined features which
distinguish it from
other clubs as well as
from hotels. It has
no bar or cigar stand,
no gambling, stock
ticker, partizan poli-
tics, sensationalism or
similar 'excitements,'
no elaborate jewelry,
toilets, display or fash·
ion; no pretentious
menu; no noise after
10 p. m.; no consump-
tivs or other guests against whom there is any reasonable moral,
social, race or physical objection; no beggars, tramps, pedlers,
'entertainers' or other solicitors, and no 'transients.' Fees and
tips are absolutely prohibited, as in all well managed clubs.
It does havė however better and stronger buildings, unusual

protection against fire,
drowning, and other acci-
dents, with organized fire
and lake patrol, sanitary
precautions that are thuro
in fact and not simply on
paper, all waste daily carried 2 miles away, absolute
cleanliness in and out of
sight, its own farms and
gardens to maintain food
supply standards, a tea
room open day and even-
ing for light refreshments,
3 libraries of over 1000
carefully chosen volumes
and 20 current periodicals,
largest variety of attractiv

High falls, Wilmington road

Club landing, St Eustace church, Mirror lake

and healthful outdoor and indoor recreations, a 'health menu' including all the most approved special foods and preparations. The great reputation is for the table, which is not that of a hotel but of a private home able to command the best in every item.   The chief distinctiv feature is provision for freedom of choice to suit various individual tastes and needs.

West from Seven Gables piazza

The club is pland specially for: 1) children and families; 2) the overworkt or convalescent needing special building up for the coming year's work; 3) the athletic who wish the best possible opportunities and facilities for vigorous outdoor life. Its standard is sumd up in the rule of the trustees that every-thing affecting health must be done and every room built, furnisht and cared for to the last detail as conscientiously as if for a private owner's most delicate child.

Club road from station

Location. The leading American authority on parks, after detaild personal inspection, said: 'It is the most attractiv location for such a private mountain park I have ever seen. I doubt if another can be found in America which combines in so small a space more attractions of moun-tain views, lakes and for-ests.' Lake Placid is gen-erally conceded to be most beautiful of the hundreds of attractiv, health-giving re-sorts in the great forest. The wonderful tonic properties of the air have given it world-wide fame as a haven for the tired and exhausted who wish to build up rapidly. Hay fever victims report it the safest refuge yet found. The Village improvement society year book, explaining its many remarkable advantages, can be had of the club secretary. Half tones[1] in this circular suggest nature's attractions about the club home.

Plant. The club has 2500 acres of grounds, golf links, for-est, fields and farms on lakes Placid and Mirror and on 5 rivers, East and West outlets, Chub, Elba and Ausable, and numerous

[1] Mounted carbon photographs may be had from the artist, C. D. Moses, Lake Placid, N. Y. or at the club: size A, 4 x 5 in. 30c; B, 3 x 9 in. 50c; C, 5 x 8 in. 60c; D, 4 x 10 in. 60c; E, 6½ x 8½ in. 75c; F, 8 x 10 in. $1; pano-rama of Mirror lake ready for framing, mat 5 x 13 in. 60c; 9 x 22 in. $2; 15 x 40 in. $7.

mountain brooks. It has many groves and woods, with camp
and picnic grounds, 3 water powers, engines, dynamo, 4 boilers,
water works and city drainage system and railroad siding for
club freight house and storage. It has new and completely
equipt central clubhouse, with 5 public and 3 private dining
rooms, 2 parlors, 3 libraries, writing rooms, 3 sun rooms,
theater, card rooms, music and dancing room, ladies billiard,
pool, writing and dressing rooms, barber shop and various other
public rooms, and 67 private rooms including 13 suites with
baths. There are 26 cottages and lodges of private rooms,

Winona wood path

with 17 free public and 25 private bathrooms, 10 tents, steam
and hand laundries, long and
short golf links with 2 golf
houses and library, livery and
private stables with box stalls,
4 lakehouses, 6 boathouses,
with motor launch and 80 row
and sail boats including canoe
house, library and 20 canoes,
31 free bath cabins, 3 farms,
3 gardens, central cold storage
and 7 ice houses, carpenter,
cabinet, paint, boat, metal
working, plumbing, blacksmith
and harness shops and other
needed buildings. Steam boil-
ers furnish ample hot water for the 42 baths and 67 lavatories,
and over 100 hot water radiators make the central houses warm
enough for the most delicate even in the coldest November
weather.   The club has in all over 80 buildings large and
small on its 2500 acres, and provides rooms, meals, horses,
boats, golf and other outdoor sports and indoor games and
amusements and whatever else is found desirable and practicable in such a vacation home.

Annual improvements. Started in a small, tentativ way
in 1895, the club has grown 10-fold in 5 years. Additions and
improvements for 1899 were more than 3 previous years
together. Those for 1900 were still more important. Work is

Peak of Whiteface

begun in the fall to insure entire freedom from noise and confusion of building operations after the season opens.

Golf and athletics. The finest mountain views of the
Adirondacks are from the club links, famous for their natural
advantages but heretofore lacking costly improvements. 80
acres were added to the first 100 in 1899. The leading Scotch
expert laid out both a 6-hole course of 1141 yards for ladies and
beginners and a 9-hole course of 3178 yards, which he
assures the club will be unexceld. Land was also bought for
extending the 9 to 18 holes as soon as needed. The greens and
lanes, water hazards and other improvements, including 2 commodious golfhouses with separate rooms for men and women,
library and writing tables, stone fireplace, kitchen, lockers, lavatories and all needed conveniences have cost, with the land,
over $20,000. The 8 Forest courts and athletic field provide for
tennis, croquet, basket and hand ball, quoits, archery, baseball,
roque, cricket, a bowling green and for other outdoor sports.
All fences have been removed and no cattle are allowd on the
200 acres set apart for athletics. A boat landing is at the foot
of the new road cut from lake to golfhouse, now reacht by
carriage roads and bicycle and foot paths from 3 directions.

Lake P

Club carry   Placid to Mirror

Boating. The club fleet of 80 small boats, now easily the best in the Adirondacks, includes 26 new boats made in the club shop and a large selection from the best American makers of guide and row boats, skiffs, gigs, paddling, sailing, canvas and birch bark canoes, working, family, sail and other favorit small boats.

Canoe club. The unusual safety of Mirror peculiarly adapts it to paddling and sailing canoes. The Morningside canoe club started in 1900 with 20 paddling or sailing canoes, nearly all new and including the best Spalding, St Lawrence, Canada, Peterboro, canvas and birch bark models. The new 2 story canoe house, 26 x 52, is specially fitted for comfort and convenience with balconies, dressing rooms, lockers, waiting room, repair shop and above the lake library with open fire.

Cooperation. This club was devised as the practical and economical solution to one of the most perplexing problems of

;rounds   from west side of Mirror lake

modern life: how to get from the annual outing the most new
strength and health for the coming year's work.   Cooperation
has solvd many other problems, and is specially adapted
to this.   Several essentials to a wholly satisfactory
summer can be controld only by some organization among
those of similar tastes and means: e. g. the house and the
people admitted, beds, table, sanitary conditions, ample piazzas
and grounds and various comforts, conveniences and amuse-

There's iron in our
   northern winds
)ur pines are trees
   of healing'

West from Pines piazza

Seven Gables   from Pine lodge

ments. In nearly every summer resort something is so unsatisfactory as to menace health or comfort or both and forbid a
return. By well-administerd cooperation much of the waste of
summer hotels can be avoided, and those wishing the same
things can get them without paying for what they do not desire.

Method and effect of cooperation. All receipts from
table, kitchen, farms, gardens, service, laundries, livery, excursions, golf, athletics and other amusements, telegraph, postoffice, barber shop, etc. are spent by the superintendent solely
to give the most possible to members. No one desires financial
profit from them. The larger they can be made each year the
better the club will be for that year. The members furnish no
capital and assume no risks of deficits. They pay a fixt price
only enough to cover actual cost of maintenance and a reasonable rent for the use of the completely furnisht plant built and
maintaind for this special use. The Lake Placid Co. is a corporation composed wholly of club members who own this plant
and furnish needed capital and assume all risks and responsibilities and accept as interest on their investment the rent
receivd from houses, rooms and boats. Members thus get the
benefit of pure cooperation without the financial risks inevitable if they ownd the costly plant, or the indefinitness if cost
were not decided till the season accounts were balanced. Thru

the advice of the council of representative members, standards and methods are made what the club as a whole prefers in its summer home.

Economy. By our cooperativ plan, members get their summer outing without business or housekeeping cares or worry, and without investment or financial liability beyond the $10 annual fee. Experience shows that average cost would be one fifth more for similar accommodations at hotels, which lack the charm of a congenial club not open to the public. This saving is possible because:

1 Prices of meals, service, laundry, livery and amusements cover only cost of maintenance thus saving usual profits, e. g. the largest and finest private baths which bring $15 a week at hotels are only $7; apollinaris and similar waters sold at hotels at 40c or 50c for quarts and 25c for pints are only 15c and 25c; messenger service usually 15c is 5c for each quarter hour.

2 Many things charged as extras at hotels are free at the club, e. g. hot and cold baths in 17 public bathrooms, excursion and picnic lunches, local, club and room telephones, 30 bath cabins, athletic fields, short golf course, 14 tennis and other courts, flowers, dark room, 20 periodicals, 3 club libraries of

West Ausable river on east road from club

Between Mirror and Placid from Mt Whitney

1000 volumes and Lake Placid library of 1300.   Paying its employees higher wages, it absolutely prohibits all fees and tips.

3 The heavy expenses of newspaper and agency advertising for guests each year are saved, as the club has in its members a permanent constituency wishing to bring or send desirable friends.   This both secures agreeable companionship and because of larger numbers reduces average expenses, thus giving all better returns for the prices fixt.

4 The half rates for rooms, baths and boats early and late keep the houses full to a degree not possible in a hotel.

5 Members, whether they come every season or not, pay the annual fee of $10 till they resign.   200 members thus pay $2000 yearly, which helps meet expenses for that season.

6 Our skilful managers understand the rare art of maintaining without lavish expenditure the high standards desired by those seeking complete comfort and freedom from petty annoyances.   Everything is bought at the lowest rates for cash, and waste, so serious in hotels, is reduced to a minimum by special efforts of the staff with the aid of the members, each of whom has a direct interest in every saving, as prices must be higher or quality poorer without such cooperation.

The Handbook explains how members can still farther reduce living expenses by building or leasing cottages or suites and owning their own furniture, boats and horses, and by complete or partial housekeeping with the privilege of buying from the club kitchen any supplies of food, cookt or uncookt. Total expenses, specially for families, can thus be made much lower than the charge for less desirable accommodations at hotels.

Membership. No one is admitted to full membership till he has spent a season at the club as an associate or guest and knows that he is in cordial sympathy with its aims and methods. No one will be receivd as a member or guest against whom there can be any reasonable physical, social or race objection. This excludes absolutely all consumptivs or other invalids

whose presence might endanger health or modify freedom or enjoyment of others. This invariable rule is rigidly enforced. See circular I on introductions.

Engaging rooms. The club is not for transient guests but is a summer home for families, open only to members and their guests. Others may be admitted for a first visit only on introduction of 2 members or on references approved by the

Clubhouse 1898

trustees. Such guests may become associates for the current season by paying the $10 fee required of all members, and have the same privileges except the right to issue invitations and privilege cards.

Rooms are not reservd for August unless as part of an engagement of 6 weeks or more, as it is manifestly unfair to turn out those wishing to spend the summer to make room for short visits at the most crowded season. Definit rooms may be reservd for 4 weeks or more if wholly in the first or second

Cascade lake on southeast road from club

half of the season; i. e. if the engagement ends by August 10, or begins not earlier than August 11. Rooms reservd for shorter periods are subject to change if necessary to accommodate those engaging for the season or completing suites, the member moved being provided with other satisfactory quarters.

Prices. Board and room in midseason is from $14 to $52.50 a week; before July 10 and after September 10, $12.25 to $31.50. These prices are made by charging meals and rooms separately. If 2 or more occupy one room it greatly reduces cost as no extra charge is made (except $1 a week for care and laundry) if an extra bed is required. Meals are at actual cost: $1.50 a day; children under 12 and maids $1 a day in the east and center dining rooms.

The standard club rooms, B, are $1.50 and $2 a day. The smaller, or C rooms, none of which have open fires or other extras, are 50c and $1 a day. The choicest and largest, or A rooms with private baths, open fires, desks, study lamps, easy chairs, couches, bookcases or other extras are $3, $4 and $5 a day. Private baths are $1 a day.

There are no transient guests or prices. For convenience the full season price is divided into days. From this there is therefore no reduction except half rates on rooms, baths and boats before July 10 and after September 10. The price of all rooms includes also privileges of the club and must cover not only care and maintenance of rooms but of the whole great estate and public rooms and various privileges free to all. (See p. 14 and 15.) There are rooms at 7 prices, from 50c to $5 a day, for those who wish to economize closely as well as for those who wish every comfort and luxury. When price of rooms is combined with meals and other things charged at cost or entirely free total bills will be found much less than for similar accommodations in hotels. Circular F, Floor plans, shows size, exposure, windows, doors, closets, fires and price of each room, house and tent.

Club's Moose island from Eagle's Eyrie, 300 acres

Invariable prices. The common hotel practice of 'charging as much as the case will bear' has never been allowd. Every room and every item of expense has its price plainly printed and this can be changed no more than the price of postage stamps. Each guest is thus sure of the most favorable terms without the humiliation of 'bargaining.'

Half rates. To induce visits out of the crowded season, rooms, private baths and boats are only half price before July 10 and after September 10.

Staff. Mr Frank A. Craig, late of the Virginia Hot Springs and the Royal Ponciana, is superintendent. Miss Maria Daniell, late superintendent of the Boston School of housekeeping, is manager, and Mrs Kate M. Jones of Paul Smith's and the Mirror Lake hotel, is housekeeper.

Season. Midseason with full staff in all departments is from July 10 to September 10. The club is open from June 1 to November 1, or 5 months each year, with as large a staff and such service as the number of members in residence warrants.

Postoffice address. From June 1 to Nov. 1 Lake Placid Club, Morningside, Essex co. N. Y.; the rest of the year, Mrs Melvil Dewey, Secretary, 315 Madison av. Albany, N. Y.

The club issues various circulars and gladly sends information to those interested, but to avoid mistakes as to what is wanted initial in list below should be used in writing for it.

O Briefest outline of objects and methods.   16 pages.

C 48 page descriptiv circular with 20 half tones.

D Distinctiv features differentiating the club from hotels. 32p.

A Amusements, recreations, cost.   Boating, golf, athletics, etc.

F Floor plans and complete price lists.   Views of cottages.

Hf Hay fever immunity.   M Members and guests, partial list.

P Half tone pictures.   I Introductions.   S Club specialties.

R Annual report and announcements to members.

H Large, illustrated, indext handbook, including all preceding.

V Village improvement society year book on Lake Placid as a summer home.   Location, climate and all details.

Whiteface from club s Moose island

Distinctiv features

The large scale of the club estate, buildings and conveniences makes it necessary to increase its present membership in order to pay expenses without raising fees or prices   The club is therefore glad to learn of new people in full sympathy with its distinctiv aims

Who ought not to come. The chief element of success in any social club is the members themselves.   But we think it a positiv injury instead of a gain to grow by accepting members not in cordial sympathy with our distinctiv features   The following frank statement is to prevent those from coming whose satisfaction is dependent on things which we do not care for and to whom the atmosphere of the club would not be congenial   One visitor wrote to a friend that he had found 'a summer resort with 3 unabridged dictionaries and no bar or cigar stand '   Some who have never made actual trial criticize the unusual club standards and hesitate to 'limit their freedom' by coming under its rules.   But in fact there are no rules, except such as all cultivated families by common consent observe.   Every one is free to do whatever he prefers as long as it does not interfere with the rights or comfort of other members   Those unwilling to accept this standard should not come to the club.

What the club does not have

The club is not a reformatory and annoys no guest as to purely personal matters not affecting others, but the atmosphere of the place is noticeably what parents prefer for their children during the formativ period.   There is no bar or cigar stand, either public or private.   No employee may use liquor or tobacco nor can either be sold anywhere on club property. Commodious piazzas and smoking rooms with open fires are provided for smokers, who as a courtesy to those who dislike smoke, refrain from smoking in parlors, libraries, ladies billiard and pool rooms or on ladies piazzas.

Sensationalism. No gambling on even the smallest scale is allowd   There is no stock ticker or Wall street reports   The telegraph and telephone offices bulletin all important news as it comes in, but horse racing, prize fighting, speculation, partizan politics and similar city 'excitements' are kept as much as possible in the background

Display. There is no respect for mere fashion. Elaborate toilets and jewelry are recognized as entirely out of place. There is no elaborately carvd, upholsterd or otherwise costly furniture, except that beds and mattresses are of the highest grade, chairs the most comfortable, plumbing and drainage the safest that our sanitary experts can provide. We believe everything fancy or extravagant out of place in an Adirondack home, and spend no money for display. Hard wood floors and rugs, as necessary for the highest standards of healthfulness, are used to the exclusion of carpets.

Elaborate menu. Our menu is much shorter than that of pretentious hotels. Each article is the best of its kind obtainable, as is the cooking, but table and service are that of a private home, not of restaurant or hotel. Meals are charged to members at actual cost, $1.50 a day. Those coming from high priced hotels often express a strong preference for the simpler club table, regardless of its lower price It aims, and experts say successfully, to exemplify the best teachings of science as to foods and their healthful and attractiv preparation. Some object to being fed scientifically because they like 'good living.' After a season at the club however they agree uniformly that they have never been at a more appetizing table, and have never been so free from the many disorders due to the defectiv quality, condition or preparation of food. The club linen, china and excellent but unpretentious service, its system of 5 smaller and 3 private dining rooms instead of the usual great hall with its noise and confusion, and chiefly the fame of its higher standards of food supplies and healthful home cooking are giving its table a reputation second to none.

Late hours. After 10 p m there is no music, dancing or other amusements or noise which might disturb those retiring early Still it is not a sanitarium. Members may sit up all night if they do not disturb those to whom the club promises entire quiet from 10 p. m. to 8 a. m.

Objectionable guests. No person is admitted as member or guest against whom there is any reasonable social, moral, race or physical objection. This excludes absolutely all consumptivs or other invalids whose presence might injure the health or modify the freedom or enjoyment of others It is useless for any sufferer from tuberculosis, epilepsy, inebriety or any contagious or offensiv disease to hope for an exception in his case because of influential friends or by paying higher prices The trustees leave the superintendent no discretion to waive or ignore their invariable rule. If thru possible misunderstanding any such guest arrives at the club, he must leave at once, as the rule will be enforced whatever the cost or annoyance. However much they regret any hardship to individuals, the trustees' first duty is to keep their pledge to members of absolute freedom from such strain on sympathies or from danger to the susceptible of possible contagion, either physical or moral, however remote.

Objectionable outsiders. No beggars, tramps, intoxicated or disorderly persons are allowd on the grounds, and no pedlers, agents or alleged 'entertainers' unless by permission of the committee appointed to protect against the undesirable solicitations which so annoy those seeking summer rest.

Variable prices. The common hotel practice of 'charging as much as the case will bear' has never been allowd Every room and every item of expense has its price plainly printed and this can be changed no more than the price of postage stamps. Each guest is thus sure of the most favorable terms without the humiliation of 'bargaining '

Transients. The club is not a hotel, does not advertise, and is not open except to its members and invited guests. There are no 'transients.' No person is admitted for even a single day for whom there have not been trustworthy introductions Presence at the club is thus in itself a voucher of character.

What the club does have

Location. It has the choicest location in the acknowledged choicest section of the entire Adirondacks, the great forest recognized more widely each year as unsurpast in all America as a summer home for either health or natural beauties.

Clubhouse 1899　　from south

Estate. Instead of the mere huge box-filled with rooms, of which many summer resorts consist, it has 2500 acres of forest, fields and farms carefully selected for this special club use after long study by acknowledged experts. These lie on both shores of 2 lakes, Placid and Mirror; of 5 rivers, East and West outlets, Chub, Elba and Ausable, and of a score of mountain brooks. It includes virgin forests and cultivated fields, woods, groves, mountains, hills, plains, valleys, ravines, glades, dingles, great rocks, high outlooks and secluded nooks, in fact almost every natural Adirondack feature at its best. This estate is treated as a private park, the forest characteristics being preservd and artificial additions avoided. Miles of ugly fence have been removed, and miles of private roads, paths and trails built. The most casual visitor to the region notices at once the charm of the grounds and their treatment.

Buildings. Its 80 buildings, large and small, have been specially built or remodeld for its use. Every detail has been most carefully studied to secure safety, health and comfort. In meeting these standards 62 buildings were torn down in the first 5 years. In place of the flimsy structures so common in 'wilderness hotels' we have more solid foundations, heavier timbers and extra bracing to secure full protection against the severe mountain storms and any possible extra load.

Fire protection. Instead of cheap chimneys with dangerous stovepipes, our chimneys run to solid foundations, are lined thruout with fireproof flues, which give better draft and protect against sparks working thru cracks where frost or wind has loosend mortar. All fireplaces and open fires have the best close fitting spark guards. The ordinary zinc or iron protection against heat is made doubly safe by free use of asbestos behind it. There are no elevators with their dangerous shafts to carry fire. Spark arresters protect chimney tops, and chemical fire extinguishers are at every needed point A 50,000 gallon fire tank was added in 1900 with 120 ft head so that the many hose lines throw water far above the highest building. Every practicable precaution is taken against the great possible danger in wood buildings. In addition a careful fire patrol is maintaind thruout the night. The club has never had a fire or serious accident and expects to maintain its record inviolate.

Fire escapes. The buildings are all low, Clubhouse, Forest, Northgate and laundry being the only ones with a 3d floor. Most rooms have 2 or more ways of egress, many of them over the upper verandas and balconies, for which the club is famous. Connecting doors are provided for emergencies at many points, and wherever necessary the most practicable fire escapes, usable by ladies or children, will also be provided.

Accidents. Similar pains are taken to prevent accidents, specially on the water. On opposit sides of the narrow lake careful men are on duty with life preservers and lines and fast boats ready for instant use. In every case these boats have reacht persons in danger so quickly that they had only a wetting instead of the serious results probable had there been no lake patrol. Any horse, harness, saddle or carriage found defectiv or worn so as to fall below our high standard is withdrawn promptly from the livery and any driver found careless is discharged.

Sanitation. In disposing of surface water, drainage and other waste, ventilation of cellars, attics and rooms, similar care is exercised. Stone walls laid in Portland cement deflect water which might get under houses and make them damp. No wood is allowd to touch the earth where it will rot. In building, the shavings and dirt are carefully removed instead of being coverd under flooring and between joists and studs where they would make a fire trap or nest for mice or insects. No tobacco chewer is employd, to cover up tobacco juice under floors. There are no cesspools, dump heaps or back doors on Morningside. The waste is carefully taken 2 miles away each night. Complete city drainage is kept in perfect repair under supervision of the most skilful experts. Everything affecting health is done and every room is built to the last detail as carefully and conscientiously as if for a private owner's most delicate child.

Furniture. The club prides itself on avoiding elaborate or needlessly costly furniture and spends little for mere 'appearance,' but it does spend much more than hotels in securing comforts and conveniences. There are plenty of bureaus, chiffoniers, rugs, reading lamps, easy chairs, couches, hassocks, hammocks, bookcases, study tables, desks and cases with draw-

ers that do not stick. If accidents happen, the club's own
cabinet-maker, carpenter, plumber or painter, living on the
grounds, can be calld by telephone and repairs made at once

Cleanliness. This essential part of health is specially enforced for everything pertaining to the table and food supplies.
We have our own farms and gardens, and thus secure a fresh-
ness and neatness impossible where market vegetables and other
supplies are 'pickt up' by pedlers and brought in to supply
'city folks,' who would never eat them if they once saw the
condition of the place from which they came. Our own shops
for all repairs and new buildings insure conscientious ob-
servance of the rules for cleanliness and safety, which could
never be enforced if the club were dependent on contractors and
outside workmen.

Comforts and conveniences. Each year the comment is
more common that the details which make life 'comfortable'
are more closely studied here than has been known before The
usual conveniences of the best hotels are in the house: Postal
ánd Western Union telegraph offices, long distance telephone to
all points, local lines to the neighboring villages, and the club
system connecting the various buildings and the higher grade
rooms, barber, hot and cold water at every turn, hot water
radiators for cool days, electric bells, etc. The club has also
a messenger service at nominal charge (5c for each quarter
hour)

Health. Instead of the traditional proprietor studying
where he can reduce expenses without being detected in lower-
ing the quality, the club was founded, built and is still ownd
and absolutely controld by those who live there with
their families. The superintendent has orders to be careful to maintain the highest standards of health, in every detail
for every room and guest, as if it were all for the largest share-
holder's own family. It is common fame among plumbers and
other workmen that nowhere else are so high standards enforced.

Tea room. This has been built for 1900 to acommodate
those who are building up strength after overwork or illness,
under orders to take certain light foods at frequent intervals,
those who chance to be away at regular meal hours and those
who would often be glad if without asking a special favor from

Club's Moose Island from Eagle's Eyrie, 300 acres

the kitchen they could order freely some light refreshments, such as tea, chocolate, cocoa, cereal or malted milk, bouillon, biscuits, cake, sandwiches, lemonade, mineral waters, ice cream and sherbet   This service, so far as practicable, will be available for private rooms, for the Winona Wood piazza, lakehouse, smokery, lake library and canoe club as well as in the private dining room in Gambrels set apart for this purpose.

Suites.   The club is built for families and consists largely of suites with parlor (usable as bedroom if wisht) 1 to 5 rooms, open fire and private bath.   These suites are often divided by 2 or more small parties wishing to be together, but the club is in fact not mere barracks of hotel rooms full of 'transients' but a collection of families enjoying home table and comforts at a minimum of cost and trouble.

Freedom of choice.   The club does not try to force each guest to use what the superintendent and trustees prefer, but follows the club rule of individual freedom in selection. Choice is offerd of single, two thirds or double iron, wood, folding, mantel or divan beds; upholsterd, box, Ideal, spiral, National or woven wire springs; hair or elastic felt mattresses; hard or soft feather or hair pillows.   In rooms or tents he can get any size from 50c to $5, any exposure, dark or very light, 1 to 8 windows, in houses with no babies under 3 years, or in houses with no children under 12, or where there are no restrictions.   He may be in the Clubhouse, or very near it, or at the ' quiet end ' of the board or gravel walks.   He may have a private dining room or table, or meals servd in his room, have all meals at the club or provide some or all at his cottage.   He may buy from the club kitchen food, cookt or uncookt, at cost of material and service, or is free to ship from home or buy of local dealers who will call for orders and deliver at his door.   His laundry may be done by best Troy steam machinery or all by hand. He may have saddle horses, buckboards, buggies, surreys, 2-wheeld carts, mountain wagons, or luxurious Glens Falls carriages; may hire or bring his own, may have drivers or, if experienced, drive himself   In boats the club has a much larger variety than any other resort.   Its 80 boats include over 20 different models and sizes so that every taste in small craft can be satisfied.   There are stone, brick and iron fireplaces, wood, coal and oil stoves, hot water and steam radiators and in 1901 electric radiators are expected to be available from the club's new power. Houses are built so as to give sun or shade, breeze or shelter, as days and moods may vary. The chief distinctiv feature of the club is this provision for varying tastes and needs of different individuals.

Amusements. The special circular A shows that the club with its long and short golf courses, the 14 courts, athletic fields and ball ground, 80 boats, canoe club and house, 3 bowling alleys, billiard and pool rooms and various other features offers a greater variety of attractiv and healthful outdoor and indoor recreations than any public hotel.

Libraries. The club has 1000 of the choicest recent books, including a special golf and outdoor library, takes 20 of the leading periodicals, and pays by the year so that every member and guest has free use of the Lake Placid library which is across the lake within 5 minutes of Clubhouse.

Besides the library in the main house there is the lake library over the water 31x62 feet, two thirds of the sides open in fair weather, all inclosed in glass for storms, with open fires for cold days. The golf library adjoining the golf house is about the same size and has similar provisions

Health menu. In addition to the regular menu the club makes a specialty of keeping on hand a large number of the modern preparations approved by physicians as specially healthful in certain cases of indigestion, overwork or other conditions where exactly the right food has been found better than any possible medicine. These include malted and cereal milk, granum, grape nuts, shredded wheat, rice flakes, granula, Uvada grape extracts, cereal coffee, cocoa shells, etc. Equal pains are taken with improved preparations of standard articles which will make them either more appetizing or more easily digested

The club nicknames are significant: ' Piazza ' club because of the lavish provision of piazzas, verandas and balconies with comfortable seats for lounging chairs and hammocks;[a] 'Nookery,' because there are so many cosy corners and card rooms where

[a] The piazza frontage is 7296 feet, or about 1½ miles, most of it 13, some over 30 feet wide; over 4000 feet is rooft.

little groups may gather by themselves, and ' Amphibians ' because as a hotel proprietor opposit said, 'those club people live half the time in the lake either swimming, rowing, paddling or sailing.' The convenient free bath cabins, swimming school and sandy beach, boathouses and docks and variety of boats lead people to use the lake 10-fold more than those at the average hotel

The distinctiv features of the club are so numerous that one must read its various publications to understand them, specially circular S on Lake Placid club specialties, and A on Amusements.

Lake Placid Club specialties

FOR CHILDREN, THE ATHLETIC AND THE OVERWORKT

The club's peculiar organization or management either excludes or does not attract certain people but it has succeeded in making a summer home at once specially adapted to each of 4 distinct classes whose needs have been tho't so different as to preclude their being supplied in any one place. Families preferring to be together often separate because they can not find a resort suited to 2 or more of these 4 groups.

1 Children who must have ample opportunity to romp, play and make just the noise that makes life miserable for those seeking quiet.

2 Athletic men, women and children whose chief need is abundant attractions and facilities for vigorous outdoor life.

3 The overworkt, nervously exhausted, convalescent and others needing the greatest quiet and rest with freedom from the usual annoyances of summer resorts.

4 Those caring most for social life and indoor amusements, music, dancing, tableaus, theatricals, afternoon teas, billiards, pool, cards, chess and numberless evening pastimes

The club recognizes that each of these features and amusements is best for some of its members and makes ample provision for all by using separate parts of its extensiv buildings and grounds so that no class shall annoy another. For the overworkt, juvenil and athletic classes provision is most unusual.

Some in each class prefer camping out while others demand comforts and conveniences of city homes. For the first there' are tents where those wishing to sleep under canvas still have

Club landing, St Eustace church, Mirror lake

the clubhouse at hand, and also camping outfits for those who wish to try roughing it with or without a guide in the primeval forest which is within walking distance on all 4 sides.

For those who demand city comforts even in the wilderness there are houses, suites and rooms of which guests often remark that equal beds, baths and conveniences are often lacking in city homes or hotels Prices for rooms or tents range from 50c to $5 a day, thus meeting every reasonable requirement.

For children there are special rooms, pavilion, playgrounds, beach, piazzas, 'Squealery,' safe boats and bathing, bath cabins, pony cart, swings, seesaws, outdoor and indoor games and sports and constant study to deserv the name 'Children's paradise' given to the club 5 years ago Without annoying adults the club by special efforts is making the ideal home for little people. One whole section of the clubhouse is for children, having a dining room with brick fireplace and radiators and a sun room 35x26, equipt specially for them and heated for cool days.

For the athletic there are mountain, forest and lake camping, climbing, walking, cycling, driving, riding, fishing, boating, bathing, long and short course golf, tennis, croquet, base, basket and hand ball, cricket, quoits, archery, bowling and other athletic games, sports, races, regattas and tournaments.

The club however not only has no game preserv, but prohibits discharge of firearms anywhere on its 2500 acres except at targets in a retired place, set apart with every precaution against accidents from chance shots. Children are encouraged to hunt small game with telescopes, which with microscopes the office lends free, and to cultivate the friendship of birds and 4-footed friends instead of killing them. Members wishing to hunt leave the club woods to those who enjoy them doubly because of their entire freedom from nimrods whose carelessness in recent years has cost so many lives.

For those needing quiet and careful building up, there are hundreds of delightful secluded nooks on the club's own 2500 acres where they may 'invite their souls and loaf'; houses to which no children are admitted; absolute quiet about buildings after 10 p m ; a table in charge of a recognized authority on dietaries who wins from those with troublesome stomachs the praise 'most appetizing table with least indigestion we have found'; library and reading rooms with the best periodicals and reference books and a large and choice collection of the most restful, entertaining and readable literature. In short, by constant consideration of their needs without intrusion of the subject, the club gives the overworkt most of the advantages without the depressing influences of even the best sanitariums.

For social life and indoor amusement the standard is that of a great private country house, and the fashionable, feverish frivolity of the typical summer hotel ' season ' is avoided. Till 10 p. m. every physical and morally wholesome indoor amusement is encouraged, and a steady effort is made to find better substitutes for much in hotel life to which careful parents object. Respect for the sabbath, early hours, and chiefly the people and atmosphere remind one constantly that the trustees aim to make the club not a summer hotel, but an ideal country home. Healthy tastes will find it equally adapted to those needing the greatest quiet and rest and to those whose overflowing vitality demands an attractiv 'something to do' for 18 of the 24 hours. Thus it is at once a paradise for athletics, for children, for collegians and other young people seeking innocent amusements, for the overworkt wishing rest and quiet, and for entire families seeking summer homes where every member can surely find many things he most values in vacation.

St Armand   Clubhouse   Edgewater road

From Forest looking north

Clubhouse from Forest 1898

Tahawus   Colden   Algonquin   Iroquois

From club golf links looking south

North from W [illegible] Club house

Between Overlook and Moose island, Lake Placid.

Part of club grounds, from west side of Mirror Lake, 1895

Lake Placid east of Overlook

Report and announcements to members

At the close of the experimental half decade which the present trustees undertook to complete, every detail of the organization, methods and aims of the club has been carefully reviewd in the light of 5 years practical experience and of the suggestions and criticisms of members and others interested. Many students of the problems of the home and of improving health and increasing working capacity by the wisest use of the summer vacation and outdoor life in the best known climatic conditions, have been attracted by the original and promising experiments of the club, and we have had the benefit of their thought and study and of much useful experiment and experience. It is most encouraging for the future to find practical unanimity on nearly every important question submitted for decision

Comparison of the members Handbook for 1900 with previous issues will show that the revision follows closely the original plan and spirit of that of 1895, changes being almost wholly in carrying out those ideas and ideals more fully as the growth of the club makes such development more desirable and practicable. Many improvements .pland from the first have been postponed till the rapidly growing numbers yielded a sufficient income to meet their cost. Others have waited till the right persons could be found to carry them out. Others are still waiting, but the actual progress during the 5 years has been greater than was thought possible in 1895. We have endured patiently many things which we wisht otherwise because the steady growth toward our ideals was as rapid as could be hoped. Without formal votes we have learnd from this experience and from scores of conferences with leading members what is preferd by most of the families who spend their summers at the club 1900 will show markt progress toward attaining these ideals.

Improvements for 1900

Superintendent. The club has been for 2 years too
large to be satisfactorily administerd without the entire time
for 6 months of each year of an expert familiar with every
detail of the work and methods of the best managed summer
and winter resorts. We have sought long for a man who had
this needed technical knowledge and experience and who
would also appreciate that the club would be largely ruind for
most of its members if it were carried on by the people and
methods and with the standards and traditions of the mere
summer hotel We found this unusual combination in Mr
Frank A. Craig, who was associated with Mr C. E Martin in the
administration of the Mirror Lake hotel at Lake Placid during
the entire period when it won its deservd eminence among the
best managed of the great Adirondack houses. Since this was
burnd in 1894 Mr Craig has been associated with the well
known leader in such work, Mr Fred Sterry, manager of the
world famous Virginia Hot Springs and also of the Royal Ponciana and of the Palm Beach inn in Florida. This experience,
with his summers at the Bryn Mawr near Philadelphia, has given
Mr Craig the best possible training for our work, in the peculiar
character of which he feels keen personal faith and enthusiasm. He took charge of the club property at the close of
the '99 season and will return from Virginia Hot Springs
and be at Morningside from May 1 to November 1 in full
charge of the current administration of the club With a competent staff of his own selection, which includes those found
most efficient in previous years, he will be responsible that all
work is done promptly, satisfactorily and without waste and
that all reasonable demands of members are courteously met

Table. Miss Daniell has been given the farther additions
and improvements she askt in the effort to make an ideal kitchen
and to maintain and improve on the high standards of the
table Besides the cold room in the house and the large cold
storage building adjoining the central ice house, a new store
room 26x35 feet has been excavated back of the kitchen.
More room has been gaind for the ranges and cellars, and
important new equipment added Sup't Craig cordially sup-
ports Miss Daniell in maintaining fully the peculiar standards

set by the club for its table, which will, at whatever cost, be held at the highest point of healthfulness.

Laundry. Both work and workers are moved from the club grounds to one large new steam laundry, 40x100 feet, just across the lake. This, in charge of an expert head laundress, is fully equipt with the best Troy machinery and steam dry-rooms It has complete housekeeping facilities and 30 rooms for the laundresses. Either hand or machine work as preferd is done promptly at reasonable prices. Smoke, dirt and noise are avoided by having the 80-horse power boilers and engines in a separate building The laundry wagon's regular trips to the club make it as convenient as before, while our grounds are freed from the chief element that mard their beauty.

Office. The club has been made a U. S. postoffice under the name Morningside, Essex county, N. Y. It has 4 mails daily, Western union and Postal telegraph offices, long distance and local telephone lines, besides a club telephone system connecting the various buildings on both sides the lake Exact astronomic time is receivd at noon daily. All A rooms in Clubhouse and Gambrels are connected by electric bells and this system or the local telephone can be extended at small cost to any cottage or tent

Change of name. With the new postoffice address we found most members wisht to keep Lake Placid in the address without awkward repetition. The vote was 4 to 1 in favor of Lake Placid Club, Morningside, N. Y. The word Park is omitted, and while Lake is prefixt, the common name will continue as from the first, Placid Club

New rules. After consultation, these new rules have been adopted as desired by most members.

1 **Firearms.** No firearms may be discharged on club grounds except at targets in places assignd, with every precaution against accidents.

2 **Use vs abuse of property.** Club furniture and other property is substantial and for use and enjoyment, not a burden to be cared for, but any abuse or injury beyond reasonable wear and tear, whether by child or adult, will be charged to the person responsible. If children or heedless adults leave books,

cushions or furniture exposed to the weather, they must pay
the damage.

3 **Freedom vs license.**   We encourage unconventional
outdoor country life with the greatest freedom consistent with
the rights of others.   If in abounding spirits some are betrayd
into anything so boisterous or unusual as to discredit the club's
good name, the superintendent has orders to exercise needed
restraint.

4 **Smoking.** Commodious piazzas and smoking rooms
with open fires are provided for smokers, who as a courtesy to
those who dislike smoke, refrain wholly from smoking in the
parlors or libraries or on ladies' piazzas.

5 **Music.** Musical instruments may be playd in the music
room, center, all lakehouses, 2 golfhouses and on piazzas, but
not in parlors, library, office or private rooms or between
10 p. m. and 8 a. m. or during the afternoon ' quiet hour.'

6 **Dancing.** Music for dancing will be furnisht twice a week
during midseason, from 8 to 10 p. m. in the music room.

7 **Evening noise.** The pianos will be closed and all noise
that would disturb sleepers stopt promptly at 10 p m

8 **Builders' noise.** No building or workmen's noise will be
allowd under any circumstances during midseason.   All con-
tracts will require completion by June 1, and unless by special
permission for emergencies no noisy work will be allowd except
between October 1 and June 1.

Children. A stone dock 50x150 feet, coverd with clean
sand, has been built on the children's beach as a playground so
that hereafter their play will not disturb the adults' piazzas or
public rooms   A children's pavilion, 26x35, has been built on
the east, and beyond it swings, tent and rooms for playthings,
tools, etc at the edge of the beautiful grove, giving so much
better facilities that neither children nor parents will object to
strict enforcement of the house rules necessary to protect those
who come for unusual quiet.   This is the new 'Squealery,' the
old one having proved too far from the clubhouse and children's
dining room.

The best juvenil books and periodicals will be added to the
club library.   As demand warrants, a traind kindergartner will
at $1 to $2 a week take entire charge of children a part of each

day in the suitable room completed for this use. Nature study under skild guidance in the fields and woods is similarly offerd We expect this experiment to prove attractiv to the children and a great relief to mothers. Prompt notice of a wish for such service should be sent.

Tutors. For those fitting for college or having work to make up, there are 2 unusually successful teachers, Yale and Williams graduates. As much work as wisht can be done under the most favorable circumstances.

Physicians and nurses. Our club is not a sanitarium but is now so large as to justify the maintenance of a model sick room for possible accidents or emergencies. Besides our expert city physician and the best local nurse retained by the club, one or more experienced traind nurses from one of the best city hospitals will be available when needed. Rooms will be specially equipt as needed for her use with various appliances seldom to be had in the country and yet important for those who wish for the sick every comfort and aid to recovery. This new feature will be specially appreciated by those who hesitate to take children or others in delicate health where they are unlikely in case of accidents or illness to secure attendants, treatment and needed appliances equal to those at home.

Library. Great need was felt in 1899 for 3 or 4 times as large a library. Changes for 1900 provide such a room, fitted with library tables, reading chairs and study lamps and kept strictly quiet. This, with 2 parlors on the dining room floor and the new office, center and music room on the ground floor, each having open fire and hot water heat, gives ample public rooms. The new library is to be not a mere collection of books and a room in which to read them, but a library in the modern broad sense including the club's whole intellectual life, literature, science, art, history and any lectures or allied work undertaken. It is not to start a summer school or bore people with efforts to 'improve their minds,' but to provide liberally for those who find in intellectual life their greatest rest and pleasure. For 1900 the library will contain over 1000 choice books carefully selected as best for club use, 20 leading periodicals, a reference library of the best general and special cyclopedias, atlases, gazetteers, indexes and dictionaries of various subjects including the leading languages, German, French, Italian, Spanish, Latin and Greek, besides of course the Century, Standard and Webster for English.   There will be 10 of the best newspapers for general use in the library.   Personal copies can be had at the office.

Besides the library in the main house there is the lake library over the water, 31x62 feet, two thirds of the sides open in fair weather, all inclosed in glass for storms, with open fires for cold days   The golf library adjoining the golfhouse is about the same size and has similiar provisions.

The club also makes an annual gift on condition that all its members may borrow from the Lake Placid public library of 1300 volumes, on the shore of the lake directly opposit. Other summer visitors pay an annual fee for this privilege

Photographs.   A library specialty will be albums containing pictures by members   A copy of anything of interest, with suitable label and date, is earnestly askt.   No other books will afford more entertainment in future years.   The club's dark room with conveniences for developing is free to all members.

Museum and zoo.   With the club's own permanent library and a suitable room we start in 1900 a club museum and ask activ cooperation from members interested in both We wish everything pertaining to the Placid section, books, pamphlets, clippings, photographs, objects of historic or scientific interest, specimens of the flora, fauna or minerals and rocks, in short anything of interest to those who love the beautiful natural surroundings which the club has chosen for its permanent home.   While we prefer the specimens labeld and mounted, everything worth keeping will be properly cared for.

Supplementing the museum we start in a small way, to be developt as interest and cooperation warrant, an aboretum with specimen trees labeld with scientific and popular names, a botanic garden for nativ wild flowers and plants, a zoo of living nativ animals, and an aquarium of nativ fish   The library will contain the best illustrated books on all these subjects, thus making the best opportunities for nature study.

We are much helpt in these new features by the fact that the state scientific officers have recognized the peculiar advantages of this township for lovers of nature who wish to study it at its best, and have had prepared by experts, bulletins with maps and illustrations on the geology, flora and fauna. All 3 can be had at the office. During each season as interest justifies there will be lectures or familiar talks illustrated by lantern slides for those wishing to know more of nature in the Placid region and to cultivate their outdoor tastes.

Gifts. Members are specially askt to make gifts to this library and museum. Being so far from large libraries we shall gladly include in the permanent reference collection any books, pamphlets or other additions which one might want during a long summer at the club.

Clubhouse. New windows make the north dining room lighter. The third story of the east wing has been changed into 2 large suites with an attractiv entrance hall. All domestics have been given rooms in their own new building and the kitchen stairs taken out, so that both floors above will be exclusivly for guests.

Tents. 6 new wall tents (one with 5 rooms) have coverd piazzas and water and drainage near at hand, thus affording every convenience to those who prefer to sleep under canvas.

Gambrels. The chief addition of 1900 will be Gambrels, now well advanced. Other proposed buildings have been postponed for a year to guard against possible accident which might delay its completion before the club opens. With its 13-foot piazza, this covers 60x100 feet. It has gambrel roof, 20-foot round corner tower, piazzas 13 feet wide on first and second and 5 balconies on third and fourth stories The 2 upper floors have 4 suites, each with parlor, open fire, private bath, rooft balcony and 2 or 3 bedrooms en suite. There are also toilet, linen room and 14 clothes closets. With hot water, electric bells, fine mountain and lake views and convenient location, these are our best suites and this is our best building.

The second floor is much larger and better than the new south dining room, so much liked in 1899. It has the round tower corner in glass, a great stone fireplace, windows with beautiful views, and balcony on all sides 13 feet wide and over 200 feet long. This is open so that direct sunlight can be admitted at all times

The entire first floor is the music room and will be the Center or general gathering place, large enough for all. The stage on the office level with wings and anterooms is 30x60 feet. Going down 3 steps lower at the curtain line a floor 32x57 seats 300 people   East and west 6-foot folding doors make a continuous promenade 13 feet wide and 60 feet long on each of the 4 sides, completely encircling the room.   On the stage level are men's and women's dressing rooms needed for theatricals, concerts and other entertainments where costumes are changed, and also for daily use of those coming from cottages to the Clubhouse, which thus has for the first time a complete ladies toilet on the lower floor At the new main entrance is a porte cochère, 17x17, with balcony seats on top overlooking the lake   Gambrels thus combines numerous markt conveniences and attractions.

Piazzas. While only 14 bedrooms are added, the public piazza space has been increast in 1900 by over 7000 square feet.   The new Gambrels has a 2-story 13-foot veranda on 4 sides   This gives sun or shade, breeze or shelter as preferd. 2600 feet east and 1560 south piazza area added this year gives sun piazza facilities unequald in this section. There is also a sun room with 6 south and 6 west unshaded windows   By an ingenious device the west piazza in front of the 2 parlors and the library (13x50) can be inclosed in glass in 5 minutes in case of wind, driving rain or unusual cold   The much prized piazza life is thus available in all weather and except when needed the glass inclosure is not seen.

Hot water heat. The clubhouse has been equipt with the most improved hot water heating system, thus preventing the otherwise inevitable discomforts of chilly mornings and nights in the mountains   There is no noise or dirt, and it admits that necessity for satisfactory summer use, slight heat under perfect control, an impossibility with steam   To this is added the charm of over 30 public and 40 private open fires so that every one can find in some convenient room a cheery blaze whenever the general outdoor heat does not forbid it.

30 of the best coal and air tight safety wood stoves arc
available for buildings not having radiators or open fires, so
that the club now has over 110 separate fires

Suites and private baths. Attractiv suites have been
added to Clubhouse, Forest, Northgate and Gambrels In
1899 19 new baths were put in and 12 more are added for
1900. These all have the most sanitary plumbing, porcelain
tubs, oval bowls with patent waste and siphon jet closets

Fire protection. 50 chemical extinguishers have been
added to the protection of the hose lines, and a careful night
watchman patrols the buildings every hour.

Golf. Over $3000 has been spent on the 9-hole 3000-
yard course. Much new work has been done under expert
advice. Most of the putting greens were rebuilt and seeded
last fall The old course has been laid out in 6 holes. This
will not be kept in as fine condition as the long course, but will
be open free to all members, and appreciated by learners who
wish to practise before attempting the regular course. The
golf teacher will also have, as in 1899, the netted inclosure for
special drill on positions and strokes. The long distance telephone lines which disfigured the links will be moved back of the
woods by May 1.

The '99 golfhouse was supplemented in November by a
second and larger one just south, with sliding doors and windows on the east and south, inclosing it in glass for chilly days
without losing any of the wonderful mountain views that have
made the first tee and home hole famous There are large
piazzas, a huge stone fireplace with adjoining room full of
wood and kindling for cold days and evenings, a ladies room
with toilet and a small kitchen with conveniences for afternoon teas or other simple refreshments This gives space to
enlarge the locker rooms for both men and women, and to
increase the golf and outdoor library so much appreciated in
1899. This will include not only the best books and periodicals
but also writing tables and stationery for those who prefer
writing outdoors in this 'Golf library '

Summer houses for shelter from sudden showers, with seats
and drinking water, will be added near the water hazards,
at Meadowbrook and on the knolls. A new trail has been

made from the golfhouses thru Lakewood tō the golf boat
landing, and platforms built for the convenience of those who
come in carriages

Rowing, sailing and paddling. The club fleet of 80 row
boats is well known as the best in the Adirondacks.   Our own
boat shop has been busy all winter building more of the finest
guide and family boats.   Over $500 has been spent on the
lakes   Placid was drawn down several feet and the East bay
in front of the club's 160-acre Maple valley, was entirely cleard
of logs, stumps and roots that made Placid's most beautiful bay
almost inaccessible.   Mirror was also drawn down, and over 100
blasts, with removal of fragments by men and horses, have
made injury to boats over the 3 sunken islands impossible
even at the lowest water.   This costly but thoro work perfects
Mirror for boating   The most fragil craft can go freely everywhere at full speed without possibility of accident from rocks
and snags, thus justifying the choice of Mirror as the best per- ·
manent course for the annual Adirondack regatta.

The new club landings for the 4 churches and the golf
links and the 9 racks added to the south boathouse will be
supplemented in May by the new north lakehouse doubling
boat storage, docks and landing, and second story public lake
library, balconies and 'smokery,' and on the lake level oar
and cushion room with lockers, waiting room, and repair shop
with experienced boat builder in charge.   100 feet away is the
new children's dock, so the noise of little people playing at
the lakehouses will no longer annoy adults

Round trip tickets on the Placid steamers Doris, Nereid
and Ida have been reduced from 75 to 50 cents each.

Bathing and swimming. The changes which have been
made give the needed space for instruction in swimming for
both children and adults, and also increase to 32 the number
of free bath cabins, all supplied with Turkish bath towels.

Canoe club. The unusual safety of Mirror peculiarly
adapts it to paddling and sailing canoes   A Morningside canoe
club will start in 1900 with the best fleet in the mountains of
20 paddling or sailing canoes, nearly all new and including the
best Spalding, St Lawrence, Canada, Peterboro, canvas and
birch bark models.   The new canoe house is specially fitted for

comfort and convenience with lockers, waiting room and repair shop

Regattas, races and tournaments. Besides the third annual Adirondack regatta the last of August, there will be frequent trial races between club houses and crews and a series of tournaments and field days to stimulate interest in the various outdoor games for which needed facilities have been so liberally provided. Members are askt to assist this movement to increase outdoor life by attracting nonparticipants to attend races, match games or tournaments

Driving. The new stable has been enlarged by box stalls and conveniences for those wishing to bring their own horses where they can have light, dry, well ventilated quarters in charge of responsible, experienced men New horses, 2 and 3-seated Glens Falls buckboards, pony cart, excellent saddle horses and other improvements add to the much appreciated club stables

Forest courts. These 8 courts in a single group were built in November, north of the baseball and cricket grounds and the Forest hole of the short golf course at the intersection of Edgewood and Midwood roads They lie east of Forest, on the trail from Seven Gables to Greenacre and the golfhouses. These give ample space for tennis, roque, basket or hand ball, croquet, quoits, lawn bowls, archery or any other games needing level turf or hard dirt courts. The east courts are shaded by Brookwood in the morning and the 4 west courts by Wayside wood in the afternoon, and the open knolls and fringes of forest trees make ideal places for seats and summer houses for those watching the games, or for protection from sudden showers. These with the Westside courts on the Mirror Lake inn property, bought last October, give 14 courts, all of which will be available as fast as needed, so that even in the crowded season there will be ample room for tournaments, matches or practice, for either experts or learners, thus affording unequald provision for the outdoor sports which the club specially aims to foster.

Excursions. Complete camping outfits are lent to those wishing to camp, picnic or climb. Walking, cycling and outdoor parties are encouraged by substantial lunches free to those absent at meal times. The cycle room is not only for storage, but for cleaning and repairs Every reasonable and practicable effort is made to increase yearly the present high standard of outdoor life and exercise which adds so much to both health and happiness

Indoor amusements. Golf, boating, driving and riding and all outdoor sports have receivd unusual attention, but provision has also been made for evenings and rainy days and for those who specially enjoy indoor recreations, and the new game room will contain facilities for all the best indoor games. The most important additions are ladies' billiard and pool tables. Photographers have a free room with the best facilities for developing, and the new music room, seating 300, with stage, curtains, dressing room, etc. provides accommodations for music, dramatics, tableaus, and entertainments for the Village improvement society or the churches.

Estate. Besides the steady work in keeping up and improving grounds, special attention is given each year to some section, rendering it more attractiv and accessible by removing dead trees, brush and waste and bringing it into the condition recommended after personal examination by our expert landscape architects and foresters This winter's work has been done on Maple valley, Moose island, Hillside farm, Meadowbrook, Lake Elba, Plains of Abraham, School st., Outlet valley and West hights Over 3000 cords of stovewood were cut, not to secure wood, but wholly to improve the grounds.

The road from Seven Gables to Moosewood has been widend, terraced and sodded and a lake path built in the trees at the water's edge clear to the lakehouse On the west side markt improvements by cutting and grading have been made and a vista opend from the new Saranac road across the lake to Morningside The shores have been greatly improved by tearing down the shabby Featherston and Forest boathouses and that greatest blemish on either lake, the 3-story Mirror Lake hotel stable.

Electric power. 2 expert hydraulic engineers find that on our Elba river, just south of the golf links (a section long wisht for, but only recently secured) we can develop 400 horse power or enough for 4000 electric lights. As soon as this is ready, probably not before 1901, it will give not only light but power for shops, heat for cottages and tents and the most perfect cooking science has yet discoverd. This will make possible many great conveniences of which the cost would have been prohibitiv had the current been bought.

Roads. The first mile of Saranac road has been built including 2 bridges over the East and West rivers. This opens a beautiful woods drive thru Outlet valley to the fine views of West hights and to attractiv walks along the wooded shores of both outlets It passes our new club water works and is only 20 minutes walk to Hillside farm When the second half is done next year, this will be the most direct road to Saranac Lake, running 2 miles from Mirror Lake inn direct to the junction of the present north and south Saranac roads.

Flower garden. For 1900 a garden has been assignd solely to flowers, free to members. Those having suggestions, or special seeds which they would like to have planted should send them promptly and the gardener will do as well as climate allows Special plots of land will be assignd on request to any members who enjoy working over flowers of their own raising.

Mirror Lake inn. The trustees in November secured the entire Mirror Lake hotel plant adjoining our Westside boathouse. This gives the much desired unbroken lake front from the Braman lot, also bought in 1899, to the Westside boathouse, with groves, and tennis and croquet courts; the best steam laundry plant in the region; 80-horse power boiler with two engines and 550-light dynamo, all in perfect order; a well equipt repair shop for water, steam and other pipes and metal work; 108 acres of land connecting West hights and Morningside and making possible our new and attractiv short road thru the woods and over the 3 rivers to the club farms. We get also the complete water works Two analyses by experts prove this water to be marvelously pure, and it is unlimited in quantity so that we shall have no farther restrictions on sprinkling dusty streets or any other free use of water. The 3-story stable on the lake side, the paint shops and old buildings have been removed, leaving only the 4-story annex, 40x100, with 30 bedrooms, boiler and engine house and large ice house. The old furniture, which of course the club would not use, has been sold, except that needed to equip the annex for the laundresses.

Farm. Besides larger and better gardens at Morningside, we have now secured Hillside farm of 220 acres selected as best for the club. This is nearest the railroad station where it has a siding and ample storage for either inward or outward freight. It has the best farm house and buildings in the vicinity, is at the intersection of the North Elba, Saranac Lake and Averyville roads, and the Chub river runs thru it, giving facilities for raising ducks and geese. Recent discoveries show that very great danger to health lurks in milk, usually without the knowledge of the seller. We have adopted the only effectiv plan to secure complete protection by having on our own farm and under constant direct supervision a carefully selected herd of choice cows which will be inspected by experts at regular intervals so that any taint can be promptly eradicated. The club's remarkably large consumption of cream and milk justifies this thoroness. Special attention will also be given to poultry, sheep, small fruits, berries and gardens The farm will be devoted solely to club use and will be steadily improved year by year with the purpose of making it a model of which the club will be proud By the new Saranac road built last fall it is only 20 minutes walk from the Clubhouse and will be a favorit stroll for the children (who will be cordially welcome) who wish to see the farm animals and methods Only by ownership of our own farm and shops can we be sure that the high standards agreed on are really maintaind and that every practicable precaution is taken for health and comfort.

Shops. A large well equipt shop for steam, water and other pipes, metal and electric work, lumber and mason yard and sheds and our own siding on 2 acres adjoining the railroad station have been added this year. With these and improved carpenter, blacksmith, paint and boat shops, the club has now little occasion to go outside for needed facilities or workmen The present complete equipment is a source of economy as well as a great convenience.

Expenses. The past year has been markt by increasing prices in nearly all directions, estimated to be 15% for club maintenance. In spite of this and the fact that most of the markt improvements for 1900 bring no direct return, prices are not increast. We rely on the larger number to divide the fixt charges so that members, instead of paying higher rates, will get more than last year for the same prices. Numerous rooms have been farther reduced in price, including all $1.25 to $1, all $3 50 to $3, all $4 50 to $4 and some 75c and $1 to 50 and 75c a day. The larger private baths, priced at $1 50 and $2, have all been reduced to $1 Meals will be $10.50 a week, and $7 for maids and children under 12 in the east or family dining rooms

The discounts have been simplified Instead of 10, 20, 25, . 33 and 50% formerly given on rooms outside 5 weeks of midseason, the half rate is extended over 2½ months and applies to boats and private baths as well as rooms but the midseason on which there is no discount is extended to 2 months This substitutes the 50% for or abolishes all the smaller discounts. There will be no charge to members or guests at the club for excursion and picnic lunches, flowers, short golf course, 14 tennis, croquet and other courts, 30 bath cabins with Turkish towels, 30 periodicals, club library, Lake Placid public library, local and club telephones, use of not less than 17 complete bathrooms and trunk and bicycle storage Many things are thus free at the club for which a charge is often made at hotels.

New printed matter. The 1900 Circular with new half
tones will be ready in April. Members should send promptly
any addresses to which they wish it maild, sending their own
cards if they wish them inclosed. New floor plans now ready
in the larger form include Gambrels and new cottages with
half tones of exteriors The distinctiv features of the club
have led many to ask fuller information The new handbook
now printing (April 6) is very fully illustrated and indext and
includes a concise history of the first 5 years, with full statement of the objects, methods, estate, buildings, equipment and
expenses Price 25c. On application single copies will be
maild free to any member or former visitor. Calendar blotters
with half tones of Clubhouse and LakePlacid, for both club
and home use of members, are ready in 4 sizes, postcard, note,
commercial and letter. Maild free.

R Supplement to annual report

Since the report was printed in March the following changes
and additions have been made for 1900. Open fires have been
increast to 70, baths to 42, lavatories to 67 and hot water radiators to 100. Ladies billiard and pool room has been bro't to
the central clubhouse New features are a tea room in the
Gambrels open day and evening for light refreshments, a barber
shop, new fire equipment with 120 ft head, 4 in supply and 12
standpipe hose lines, doubling fire protection of corridors,
telephones in A rooms, 5 baths in Seven Gables and 4 in Forest,
hot water in Wayside, new porch to Clubhouse, with balconies
from rooms 3, 11, 37, 43 and 44, children's pavilion 35x26
inclosed with sliding glass doors and heated for cold weather,
private office for superintendent, new cellar and store rooms
under old Clubhouse, new chimneys, new piazzas, trunk and
bicycle rooms on office floor, road widend, grounds graded,
stone walls at Clubhouse and Wayside replaced with sodded
terrace like Forest, new lake library 26x52 with 4 balconies
inclosed with sliding glass doors and connecting with old lakehouse, messenger service establisht for all cottages at only 5c
for each quarter hour or fraction. A second farm (Highland)
with complete equipment has been bo't adjoining Hillside
farm; the house of 11 rooms, in excellent condition and very
comfortable, has been renovated and fitted for housekeeping
and added to the available club cottages for those who wish
retirement, ample room and low rent. The old buildings which
disfigured the north end near Northgate and Woodside have
been replaced by an attractiv cottage, and Outlook, the latest
and most picturesque club cottage, has been completed among
the pines east of Wayside. In Valley Forge a new dry kiln for

lumber, holding 50,000 ft, is in use, and a new stable will supplement present outgrown accommodations. Baygrove, the old Squealery, has been made into rooms, 3 on 1st and 5 on 2d floor   Garden has a second brick fireplace and its south piazza enlarged, with other improvements. The children's dock, 50x150, has been built out by solid stone filling so that its 13 ft board walk between the water and the inclosed sand playground, with the extension across the boat landings, gives over 400 ft of broad promenade at the water's edge.

Changes in Gambrels

Since the first proofs were printed from the architect's drawings important changes have been made in this building, as shown in the new plans and prices as actually printed Among these additions are a north balcony 13x60 ft, on the east a balcony 15x40 ft, reacht by French windows from the hall and 3 rooms, and a third balcony on the south. Some of the private balconies are fitted with casement or slide windows so to be converted into sunrooms if wisht.

There are larger rooms and closets, more windows, French windows opening to private balconies from nearly every room, private telephone in each room and in the corridor general telephone for longer distances; hot and cold running water at 11 points, 10 lavatories, with bitransit wastes and double basin cocks enabling one to wash in running water at any temperature, solid porcelain tubs in all 4 baths, 6 stone and brick fireplaces, ample hot water radiation, complete lavatories in recesses in 4 rooms not opening out of baths. The top floor ceiling has been raisd 2 ft, and 6 ft trunk room and air space thuroly ventilated by 8 louvers built.

On the dining room floor have been added 3 private dining rooms, a tea room open day and evening, and a coat room, on the office floor, ladies billiard and pool rooms and club barber shop.

Obviously these important and costly additions made necessary some increase in prices. The 2 sleeping floors are made the same price and most people will prefer the upper because of the 2 ft higher ceilings, greater quiet and finer views. Window awnings are provided wherever needed and the furniture is all new, of the best A grade, and includes in all rooms where wisht couches, desks or study tables, extra bureaus or chiffoniers. The rooms have been pronounced by all who have seen them better than any others yet built by any summer resort in the Adirondacks   Except the 4 south corners, which are $4 and $5, these 10 choicest rooms on the grounds are all $3 each.

Floor plans and prices

To guard against possible misunderstanding the secretary signs and sends for every engagement a card stating exactly what has been engaged, with room numbers as on these floor plans, time of arrival and departure and total price by week. A printed copy of the club's invariable rules by which bills must be settled, accompanies and is made part of each engagement. For explanation of club plan of prices see Circular or Handbook, p. 14-19.

There are no transient guests or prices. For convenience in bills the full season price is divided into an even amount for each day. From this there is therefore no reduction except half rates on rooms, baths and boats before July 10 and after September 10. This price of rooms includes not only rent, care and maintenance of rooms but also all club privileges, and must cover the pro rata cost of the whole great estate and of public rooms and various privileges free to all. (See Circular p. 14, 15.) There are rooms at 8 prices, from 50c to $5 a day, for those who wish to economize closely, as well as for those who wish every comfort and luxury. Combining price of rooms with that of meals and other things charged at cost or entirely free, experience shows that average bills would be about a fifth more for similar accommodations at hotels, which also lack the charm of a congenial club not open to the public.

RF30N31Mr1

Lake Placid Club   Lake library, canoe and boathouses and lakeside dining rooms

Lake Placid Club Lakeside dining room, lake house and library from forest

Lakeside Clubhouse. A rambling, picturesque building,
covering an acre, with 77 sleeping rooms, 6 dining rooms,
parlors, library, office, writing and billiard rooms and large
amusement hall with stage for music, dancing, amateur plays,
etc. 3 public baths, shower bath, 12 toilets and 13 suites
of various sizes with private baths. 985 ft of piazzas and
balconies, several of which may be quickly inclosed with glass,
making sun rooms for cool or windy weather. Several rooms
opening on halls are used for writing, reading and card
parties by those rooming near. The Squealery or children's
pavilion, 26x35, is on east end. This first clubhouse is so
built on side hill that each of 3 stories may be enterd from
ground level. At the porte cochere the lawn is on the office
level. At the parlor entrance, on the dining room floor, it is a
story higher. On the east one walks from the lawn on to what
is 3d story in front. This adds not only to picturesqueness
but greatly to comfort of those who dislike stairs. The entire
house is heated by 100 hot water radiators from twind boilers
of unequal size. In mild weather the small, in colder the
large, and in coldest both boilers are connected with each
radiator. This is the most perfect heating system known.
Hardwood floors, 23 open fires, 17 brick and stone fireplaces,
9 in public rooms, 8 in suites.

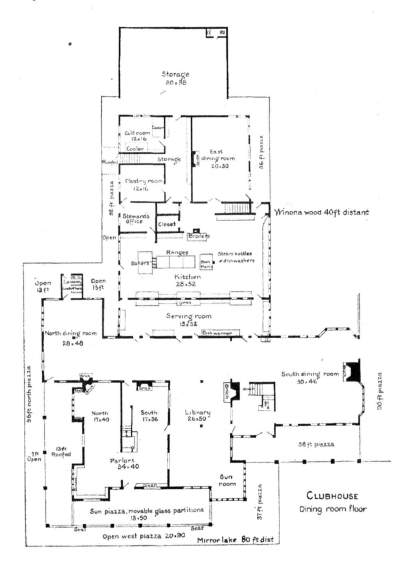

Storage
80 x 56

Cold room
12 x 16
Cooler
Stair
Storage

East
dining room
20 x 30

36 ft piazza

52.4 ft piazza

Roofed

Pastry room
12 x 16

Winona wood 40ft distant

Stewards
office
Closet
Broilers

Open

Bakers
Ranges
Room
Pantry
Steam kettles
+ dishwashers

Kitchen
28 x 52

Open
13 ft
Lavacem
Coats+hats
Open
13 ft

Serving room
13 x 52

Urns

Dish warmer

North dining room
28 x 48

96 ft north piazza

Brick

South dining room
30 x 46

90 ft piazza

North
17 x 40
Brick
South
17 x 36
Library
26 x 50
Brick
down

7 ft
Open
13 ft
Roofed

Parlors
34 x 40

Sun
room

58 ft piazza

37 ft piazza

Brick

Sun piazza, movable glass partitions
13 x 50

Seat
Seat

Open west piazza 20 x 90   Mirror lake 80 ft dist

CLUBHOUSE
Dining room floor

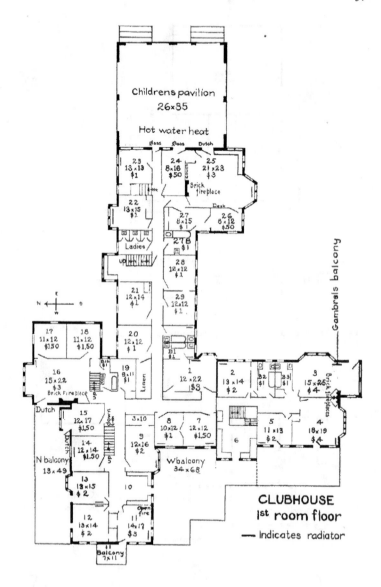

Childrens pavilion
26×85

Hot water heat

CLUBHOUSE
1st room floor

— Indicates radiator

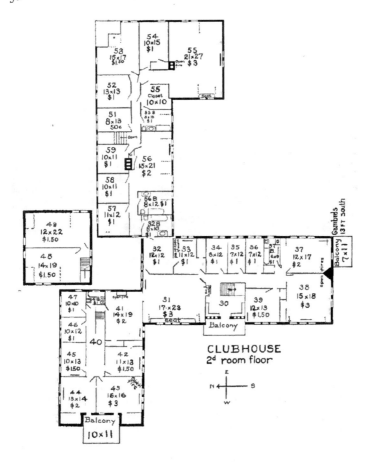

CLUBHOUSE
2d room floor

Lake Placid Club   Lakeside dining rooms, lakehouse and library   from west   400

Gambrels. This south wing of Clubhouse was built in 1900 and has 2 floors of the largest and finest suites, with private baths, in the Adirondacks. The tower sitting rooms are 22x25 ft with 7 windows commanding fine lake and mountain views, brick fireplaces, desks, couches, easy chairs and every convenience. The plumbing is the best, only solid porcelain baths and slop sinks being used. The Gambrels dining room on main house level is specially attractiv, with windows on 3 sides, stone fireplace, hot water heat and large tower circle. It also serves to deaden any sound which might come to upper floors from music room beneath. Tea room and private dining rooms are on 2d floor. Barber shop, billiard and pool rooms, stage and music room, long distance telefone booth and center on 1st floor. Hardwood floors, 6 brick and stone fireplaces.

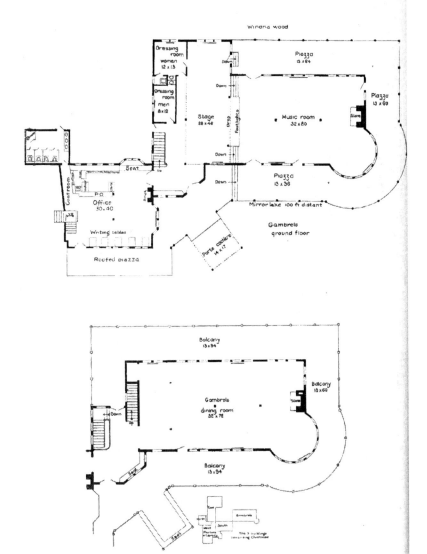

Seven Gables 300 feet south

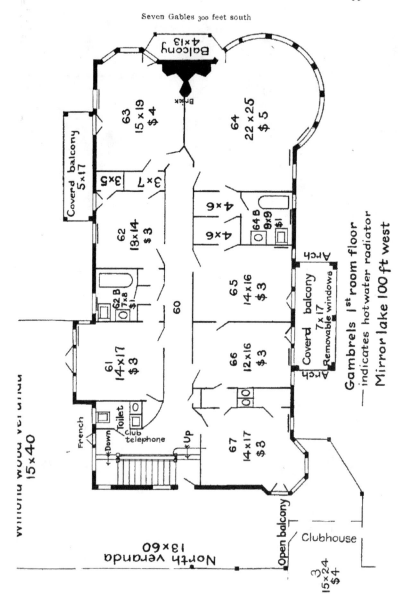

Balcony 4x13

63
15 x 19
$4

Brick

64
22 x 25
$5

Coverd balcony 5x17

3x5

3x7

4x6

4x6

64 B
9x9
$1

62
13x14
$3

65
14x16
$3

Arch

62 B
7x8
$1

60

Coverd balcony
7x17
Removable windows

Arch

61
14x17
$3

66
12x16
$3

Arch

French

Toilet

Club telephone

Down

Up

67
14x17
$3

Window wood veranda
15x40

North veranda
13x60

Open balcony

Clubhouse

3
15x24
$4

Gambrels 1st room floor

— indicates hot water radiator

Mirror lake 100 ft west

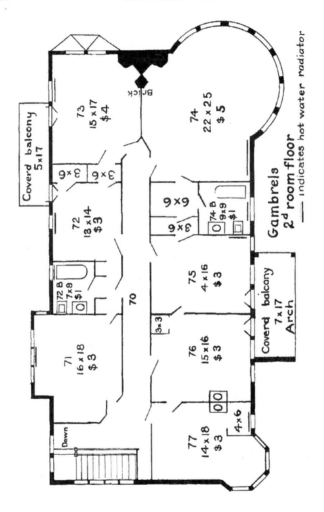

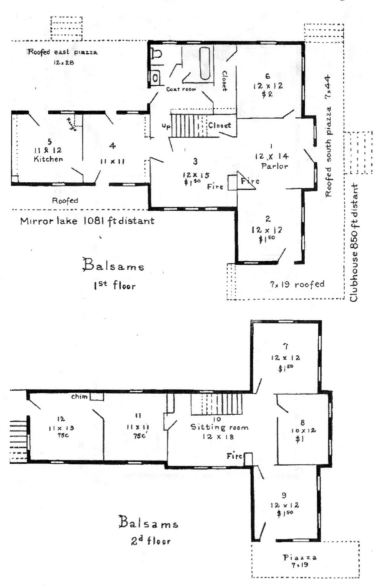

Roofed east piazza
12 x 28

Coat room

Closet

6
12 x 12
$2

Up

Closet

5
11 & 12
Kitchen

4
11 x 11

3
12 x 15
$1⁵⁰

Fire

Fire

1
12 x 14
Parlor

Roofed

Mirror lake 1081 ft distant

2
12 x 12
$1⁵⁰

Roofed south piazza 7 x 44

Clubhouse 850 ft distant

Balsams
1ˢᵗ floor

7 x 19 roofed

7
12 x 12
$1⁵⁰

chim

12
11 x 13
75c

11
11 x 11
75c

10
Sitting room
12 x 18

8
10 x 12
$1

Fire

9
12 x 12
$1⁵⁰

Balsams
2ᵈ floor

Piazza
7 x 19

Balsams. 3 minutes east from Clubhouse, on the summit, picturesquely located at highest point of park over 100 ft above lake and therefore commanding the broadest views. 12 rooms besides bath, 3 open fires, hot and cold water, complete kitchen equipment, separate stairs and plumbing for servants, large stable, ice house and 3 acres of lawn and grove. Day's rent $10.50, year's $735.

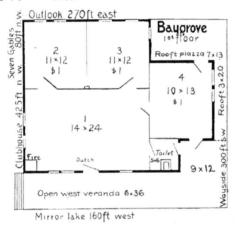

Baygrove. Rustic, bark exterior, 2 minutes south from Clubhouse, in east edge of evergreen grove on bay between Seven Gables and Wayside. Shaded only on west. Running water, toilet, no bath. Formerly children's 'Squealery.' Rebuilt in 1900. Day's rent $7, year's $490.

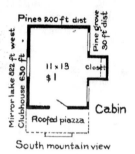

Cabin. Rustic lodge, bark outside, furnisht and cared for like a Clubhouse room. South of Pines, 176 ft east of Pine lodge, 3 minutes from lake, 2 from Clubhouse, in edge of beautiful grove. Free from noises of even a small house. Day's rent $1, year's $70.

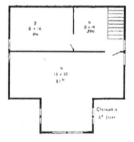

Clematis. Red cottage, on lake front, second south of Forest, 4 minutes from Clubhouse. Running water, drainage, no bath. Closet and hot water in annex 30 ft from east door. Simple camp construction. Day's rent $5.50, year's $385, either with care or furnisht for simple housekeeping.

Colden and **Eastgate.** 2 small cottages for housekeeping on east edge of golf links half mile from Clubhouse. **Edgehill,** the best of the club's farmhouses. Also several other housekeeping cottages at a distance from club. For plans and prices see supplement.

Edgewater   from northwest

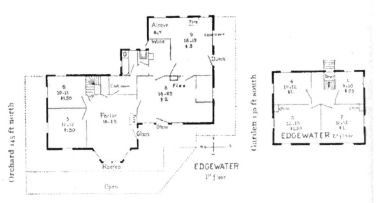

Edgewater. 409 ft or 1⅓ minutes north from Clubhouse.
Low ceilings sloping on 2d floor.   Quiet, with beautiful
glimpses of mountains and lake thru pine trees.   Red, winter
house, cellar, plasterd and paperd. except o which, having no
room over it, is ceild in spruce into peak.   2 open fires, water
on both floors. Day's rent $12.25. year's $857.50.

Lake Placid Club   Forest   from west   395

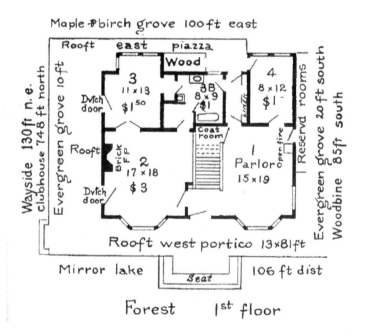

Maple ⊕ birch grove 100ft east

Rooft   east   piazza

Wood

3
11 x 13
$1.50

3B
8 x 9
$1

4
8 x 12
$1

Dutch door

Rooft

Brick F P

2
17 x 18
$3

Dutch door

Coat room

Parlor
15 x 19

open fire

Evergreen grove 10ft

Wayside 130ft n.e.
Clubhouse 748 ft north

Evergreen grove 20ft south

Reservd rooms

Woodbine 85ft south

Rooft west portico 13 x 81 ft

Mirror lake   Seat   106 ft dist

Forest   1st floor

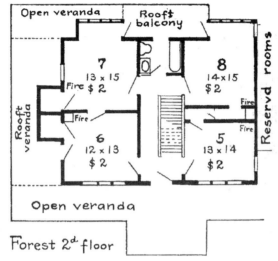

Forest 2ᵈ floor

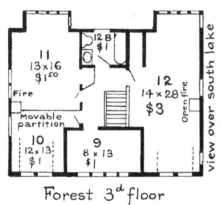

Forest 3ᵈ floor

Forest. On choicest site, on knoll 30 ft above lake, directly opposit finish of regatta courses. 3 minutes from Clubhouse. Finisht August 1899. Green, winter house, hardwood floors, fine cellar, 4 baths, hot and cold water on all floors, coal heater for cool weather, 1 brick fireplace and fires in 9 other rooms. 10 and 11 are in 1 room but will be separated as in plan if preferd. Day's rent 1st floor, 2, 3, 4 and bath (parlor free) $6.50; 2d floor (bath free) $8; 3d floor, 4 rooms and bath, $7.50.

South wing, 5 rooms, bath, wood and storerooms, fully equipt for housekeeping, is omitted on plan, being used by club officers. It has separate stairs, piazzas and 4 outside doors, so is really distinct building but is used conveniently with Forest in winter.

Garden   from south

Casement
4
13×14
Casement $1.50

Open
5×8

Alcove
8×8

Brick fireplace
5
13×22
$3

Dutch

Casement

Wood O

Rooft piazza
12×18

Slide door
8×9

5 B $1

Open 3×22

3
10×11
$1

Glass
8×9

6 clos.

down

UP

Fire

6
16×18
$3

Brick

2
12×14
$1.50

1
Parlor
14×17

Rooft
piazza
7×16

Open
12×23

Edgewater 130 ft north

Open 3×32

E

N   S

W

Rooft piazza
13×34

Mirror lake 158 ft west

Tennis court

Clubhouse 212 ft south

GARDEN
1st floor

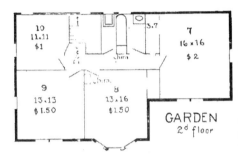

GARDEN
2ᵈ floor

Garden. Brown, winter house, large cellar, behind the great pines, 1 minute or 212 ft north from Clubhouse. Flat roof, high ceilings, 2 brick fireplaces. Like Winona, each floor, having hot and cold water and bath, is an admirable suite for a family. Very high ceilings in 7 and 9 which, having no rooms over them, tho on 1st floor, are ceild into peak. Coal heater between 7 and 9 heats water without warming house. When wisht this heat can be turnd on rooms. 1st floor (parlor free) day's rent $11, year's $770; 2d floor (bath free) day's $6, year's $420. .

Lake Placid Club   Hillside   from Southwest   490

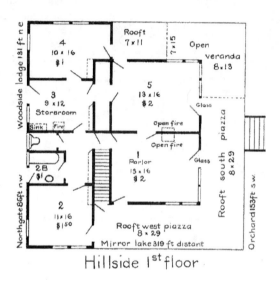

Hillside 1st floor

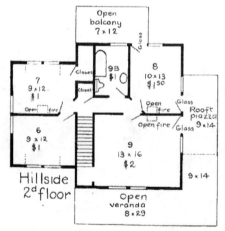

Hillside 2d floor

Hillside. Built in 1900 as 2 separate suites, each floor having parlor, 3 bedrooms, hot water, bath and open fires, 2 on 1st and 3 on 2d; 1st floor has also heat and storeroom which may be used for light housekeeping. Hardwood floors, good cellar. Piazzas on 3 sides on 1st floor and 3 balconies on 2d, rooft on south. Brown clapboards 1st story, cedar shingle, natural finish, on 2d. 3 minutes from Clubhouse, 1 minute from lake, near Northwood. 1st floor, day's rent $7.50, year's $525; 2d floor, day's $6.50, year's $455.

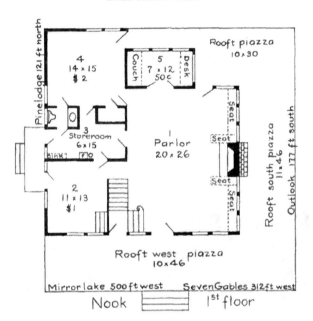

Nook   1st floor

Nook   2d floor

Nook. Rustic cottage, bark exterior, just beyond Pine lodge in half circle of beautiful pines open to south mountains, will be completed June 1, 1901, for the *Outlook* staff, for whom it was pland and built. 2 minutes from Clubhouse, 1½ from lake. Room 3 can be used for light housekeeping. Hardwood floors, stone fireplace, 4 open fires, bath, hot water and toilets on each floor.

Lake Placid Club   Northgate   from northwest   429

Northgate. Green, winter house near north boundary of Morningside, 1 minute from lake front, 2½ from Clubhouse. Bath, 2 closets, hot and cold water on both floors, 3 open and 6 other fires, parlor, kitchen, 11 large bedrooms, large cellar, private boat house, ice house. Best for housekeeping for large party, using 2 as kitchen. Beautiful grove on lake shore 100 ft west, extensiv forest 50 ft north. Open to sun on east and south, large piazzas on 4 sides, balconies on each floor. Very quiet, roomy and convenient.

11, 12, 14 and 15 are in completely separate building, having independent stairs, piazza and toilet. Day's rent $3.50, year's $245. Main part alone $13.50 a day, $945 a year.

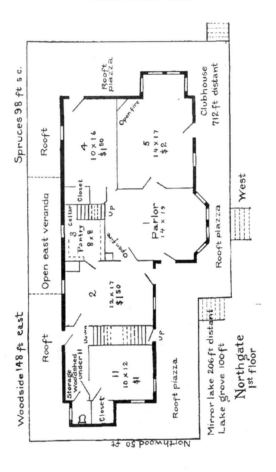

Spruces 98 ft s e.

Woodside 148 ft east

Roof

Open east veranda

Roof

Closet

Pantry
8 x 8

Cellar

Closet

UP

Open fire

Roof
piazza

4
10 × 16
$1.50

5
14 × 17
$2

Parlor
14 × 19

Clubhouse
712 ft distant

Roof piazza

West

Open fire

Down

UP

2
12 × 17
$1.50

Storage
woodshed
under 11

Down

Closet

11
10 × 12
$1

Roof piazza

Roof

Mirror lake 206 ft distant
Lake grove 100 ft

Northgate
1st floor

Northwood 50 ft

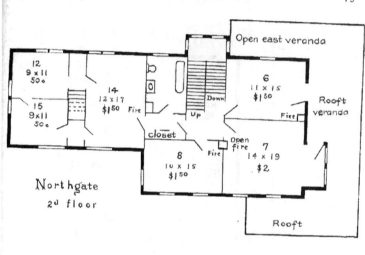

Northgate
2ᵈ floor

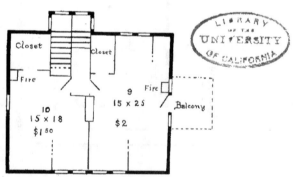

Northgate 3ᵈ floor

North lakehouse. Upper story, 16x20 ft, with balcony over lake, is a delightful retired room. 1st floor toilet at Northgate, 1 minute distant. Day's rent $2, year's $140.

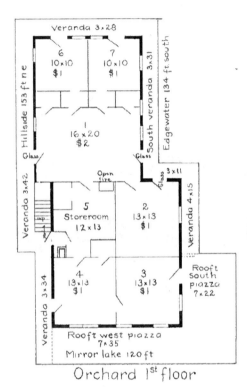

Orchard 1st floor

Orchard. Rustic camp construction, bark exterior. On lake front between Edgewater and Northgate. Having outside stairway and distinct entrances below it may be used by 1 family or as 3 separate suites. Hot water, open fire. Toilet on 1st floor, bath on 2d. 1st floor, day's rent $7, year's $490; 2d floor, day's $5.50, year's $385.

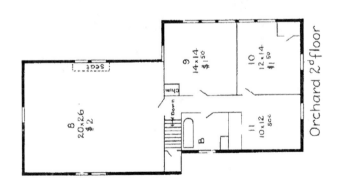

Orchard 2d floor

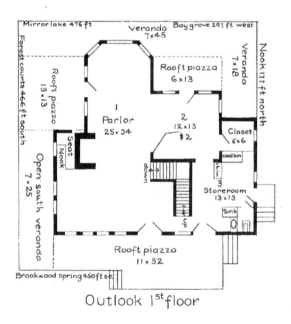

Outlook 1ˢᵗ floor

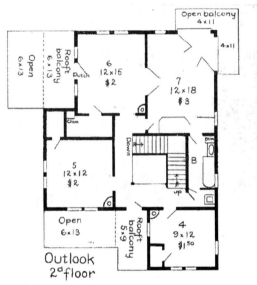

Outlook, 3d floor, 13x13, $1.50

Outlook. Built in 1900 for L. E. Waterman. Shingle sides. Large, glass inclosed outlook on 3d story commands fine views. 3 piazzas, 3 balconies, 1 entire corner opens so to throw room 7 into balcony. Hot water and toilets on both floors, bath, cellar, heat room, butler's sink. Coal heater, brick fireplace, hardwood floors. 2½ minutes from Clubhouse, 1½ from lake, 1½ from Forest courts.

Pines   from south

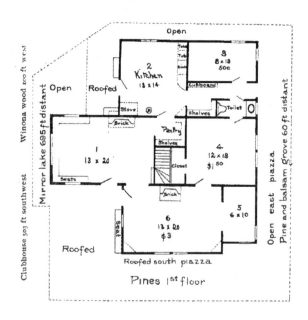

Pines 1st floor

Pines. Red cottage on summit, 3 minutes from lake and 94 ft above it. Finest views in Placid region. Parlor, alcove library, dining room, 6 bedrooms, bath, toilet rooms with hot and cold water on both floors. Hardwood floors, venetian blinds, 4 brick fireplaces, completely equipt kitchen, set laundry tubs, pantry, refrigerator, large separate ice house, attic, trunk room, 600 gallon copper lined reservoir. 200 ft of piazza, on west 15 ft wide, surrounds entire house. Under it are wood and store-rooms with 3 outside doors. Study windows command finest east, south and west views of forest, lake and mountains. On the 6 acres are 2 beautiful groves, tennis court, stone camp-fire, boat house and dock. Day's rent $12.50, year's $875.

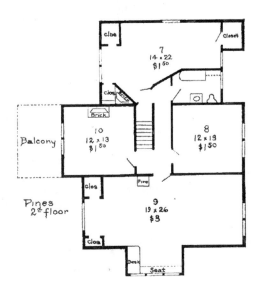

Pine lodge. Picturesque little house in natural wood inside and out, 2 minutes from Clubhouse, 550 ft from lake. Named from great pines which rise thru piazza floor and make a thick foliage roof to an outdoor sitting room. Coverd outlook

Lake Placid Club   Pine Lodge   from west   431

on roof among pine branches, with seats for 8, is reacht by
stairs from piazza extending round entire building. Toilet
with running water, lavatory and closet. Woodshed under
parlor and piazza is reacht by outside door, or in rainy weather
by inside trap door. Window seat lounge, open fire, closet, 3
single beds. Couch in recess gives no suggestion by day that
parlor at night is extra bedroom. Large casement windows
frame most beautiful south mountain view. West windows
command both lake and mountains. Finisht in natural wood
into gambrel roof. Book shelves and writing desk built in.
Day's rent $3.50, year's $245.

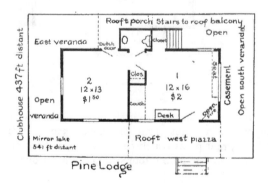

Pine Lodge

Seven Gables   west piazza

Seven Gables. Brown house on lake front, 1 minute from new Gambrels dining room thru Winona wood path. West gables 4–8 and 17 to 19 is winter house, plasterd and paperd, with cellar. North and south gables 1–3, 9, 12–16, 20, 21, for

West from Seven Gables piazza

Baygrove 80 feet s. e.

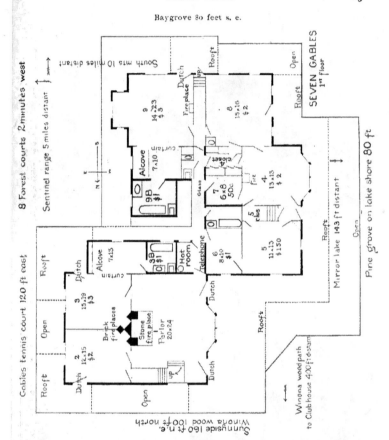

fall use, have natural spruce finish. No children under 12 ever room here. 6 open fires, 1 stone and 2 brick fireplaces, 5 baths, toilets and lavatories, hot and cold running water on both floors, coal heater to temper north wing in cool weather. Most general favorit among club cottages.

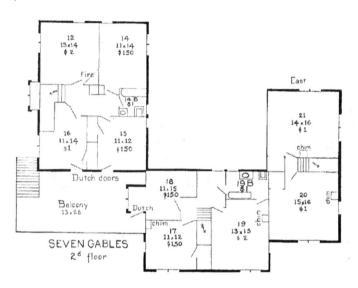

SEVEN GABLES
2^d floor

Seven Gables   back view from Pine lodge

Sunnyside 1st floor

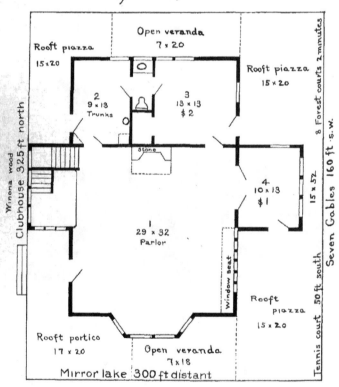

Open veranda
7 x 20

Rooft piazza
15 x 20

Rooft piazza
15 x 20

2
9 x 13
Trunks

3
13 x 13
$ 2

Stone

4
10 x 13
$ 1

1
29 x 32
Parlor

Window seat

Rooft
piazza
15 x 20

Rooft portico
17 x 20

Open veranda
7 x 18

Mirror lake 300 ft distant

Clubhouse 325 ft north

Winona wood

8 Forest courts 2 minutes

Seven Gables 160 ft s.w.

15 x 52

Tennis court 50 ft south

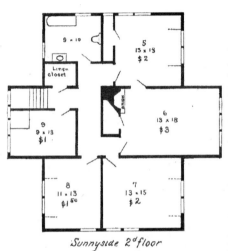

Sunnyside 2ᵈ floor

Sunnyside. Open to sun on east, south and west, touching Winona wood on north; natural cedar shingle finish. Fall construction, double ceild and paperd but no cellar or plaster. 1 minute from Clubhouse or lake. Largest parlor and bath on grounds. Hardwood floor, 1 brick and 1 stone fireplace, coal heater with registers in bath and upper hall to temper house on cool days. Bath, hot and cold running water on both floors

Best type of club cottage.   Day's rent $12.50, year's $875.

Thenagen.   See supplement.

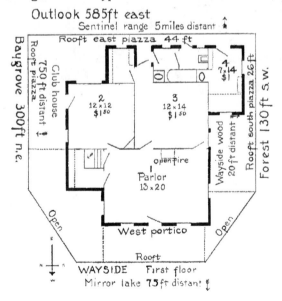

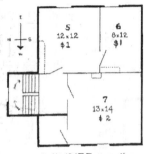

WAYSIDE 2d floor

Wayside. Brown, winter house, fine cellar, 2½ minutes from Clubhouse on knoll 20 ft above lake, with beautiful lake and mountain views. Bath, hot and cold running water, 2 lavatories, 2 open fires. Day's rent $8, year's $560.

Westside lakehouse

4 large corner rooms about 12x18 fill whole top floor, with running cold water and drainage and 2 open fires. Toilet and lavatory on floor below. On lake shore at end of club estate, directly opposit Clubhouse, from which it is 5 minutes row across lake or 10 minutes walk thru Westwood. Used usually by college men who prefer the larger rooms and do not mind greater distance. Cared for by club chambermaids. East rooms over lake $1.50 each, west rooms over grove $1.

Winona   back view from south

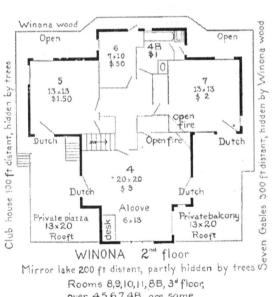

WINONA   2nd floor

Rooms 8,9,10,11,8B, 3^d floor,
over 4,5,6,7,4B, are same
size and price.

Winona. The 'house in the woods' ½ minute south from Clubhouse and east from lake. Shingled outside, natural wood inside Flat roof, 4 large rustic, rooft balconies among the pines and balsams, which almost touch it on all sides. Much direct sun comes over and between trees thind out for the purpose. Hot weather favorit. 2 baths, hot and cold running water on both floors, 4 open fires, coal heater in basement with registers to warm halls. Nearest Clubhouse, yet very quiet Same bellboy service as main house. The 2 floors are 2 entirely separate suites, each with parlor, 3 bedrooms, 2 open fires, private hall and bath and 2 rooft balconies. Day's rent of each suite $8, year's $560.

1, 2 and 3 are on west side ground floor. 1 has north and west windows, 2 has double glass doors and west windows, 3 has south and west windows All have large closets and outside glass doors Woodroom, 2 closets, hot water heater and air space are between east bank and these rooms, to protect against dampness All 3 open also into hot room. Because of prejudice against rooms near ground prices are less than half, or 50c each

Woodbine Red, summer cottage, next south of Forest, on lake front, 3 minutes from Clubhouse. Camp construction, no plaster. Stone fireplace, running hot and cold water and toilet but no bath. For housekeeping 2 is dining room, 4 kitchen. Day's rent $6.50, year's $455

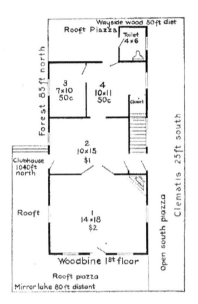

Wayside wood 50ft dist

Rooft Piazza

Toilet
4×6

Forest 85ft north

3
7×10
50c

4
10×11
50c

Closet

Clematis 25ft south

2
10×15
$1

Clubhouse
1040ft
north

Rooft

1
14×18
$2

Open south piazza

Woodbine 1st floor

Rooft piazza

Mirror lake 80ft distant

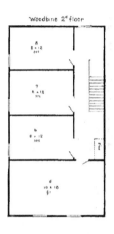

Woodbine 2d floor

8
8×12
50c

7
8×12
50c

6
8×12
50c

5
10×18
$1

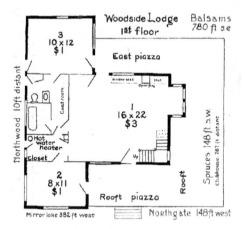

Woodside Lodge 2ᵈ floor

Woodside lodge. Built in fall of 1899. At extreme north or 'Rest end' of club estate where there is almost no passing. Red, clapboard and shingle exterior. 3 minutes from Clubhouse, 1½ from lake, in edge of Northwood. East, south and west open to sun. Hardwood floors, hot and cold running water, bath, open fire, coal heater to temper house nights and cool days. Cosiest and quietest. Day's rent $7, year's $490.

Tents. There are 1 family (5 room), 8 large (14 x 17) and 1 smaller (10 x 10) wall tents on firm wood floors with 6 ft piazzas full width of tent. Canvas flies over both tent and piazza protect from rain and sun. Larger than rooms at same price and have same furniture and care. Quieter, each tent having entire site to itself. Morningside being private park with night watch patroling every hour, ladies often room in tents alone and there has been no case of annoyance or fear. Physicians often prescribe sleeping in tents because of fresher air. Most people are surprised and delighted with comforts and advantages on trial. They are much warmer than expected in cold weather, cooler in hot, and freer from dampness in heaviest rains. Every tent stands as high and dry above the ground as a house, with free circulation of air under its wood floor, and has an oil stove which readily raises temperature when wisht, or a small iron stove with pipe running thru opening in canvas can be set up.

No baths or plumbing but all tents are within 1 or 2 minutes of club toilets and at various points running water and drainage are provided, thus adding greatly to convenience. Many who have tried it will not take rooms in houses if tents can be had   Tents are often located in some favorit spot specially chosen by the occupant   They are usually named from nearest cottage, but not because connected with it, tho often used by the same party.

While tents cost less to build than houses, furniture is same, care for chambermaids double because of distance from linen room and supplies, and each occupies a whole site.

The large tents (14x24)[a] are $1.50 a day, the same as regular rooms.   Smaller tents (10x16) $1; smallest size (10x10) 50c.   Family tents with 4 corners cut off as 4 bedrooms, 8x8, center as sitting room, with piazza under fly at both ends making long room 10x29 feet, $2.   Other tents can be put up on a week's notice on any approved sites.   Present tents stand as follows:

Cabin tent (10x16) just east of Cabin in edge of pine grove, $1.

Cherries tent on hill 400 ft from Clubhouse and 200 from Pines.   Beautiful view.   On north edge of Winona wood Family size, 4 bedrooms 8x8 and sitting room 10x29, $2

St Armand and Pavilion tents (14x24) stand together 80 ft from children's pavilion, 80 from Winona and 150 from east entrance to Gambrels. $1.50 each.   .

Winona, Sunnyside and Seven Gables tents (14x24) stand near each other in Winona wood centrally between these 3 cottages, about 200 ft from Seven Gables and 100 from Winona, Sunnyside and Gambrels. $1.50 each.

Idlewild and Waneka tents (14x24) in grove of great pines, 300 ft east of Seven Gables, 100 southeast of Pine lodge, 150 southeast of Sunnyside, 200 north of Outlook and 400 southwest of Clubhouse. $1.50 each.

---

a In all these measures platform is included, as it is coverd by fly. To get size of walls of tent alone deduct width of piazza, 6 ft from larger number.

Adirondack Lodge. Forest branch of club, 10 miles from main Clubhouse, on Heart or Clear lake, noted as largest log house in world. 3 stories, with high tower commanding magnificent mountain views. There are besides the Lodge, shown on plans, 16 other buildings, stables, boat houses, laundry, men's, women's and guide's camps, theater, lodges, cottages, tents, day camps, tennis and roque courts, etc. 50 miles of trails have been cut from the Lodge direct to the most famous peaks, passes, waterfalls, and other natural features which cluster about this remarkable spot.

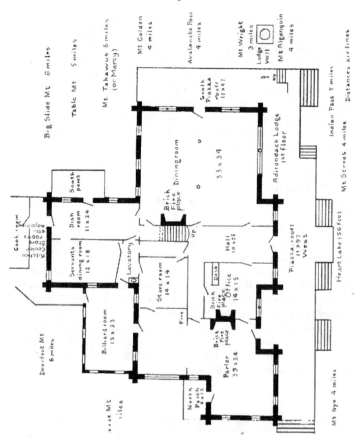

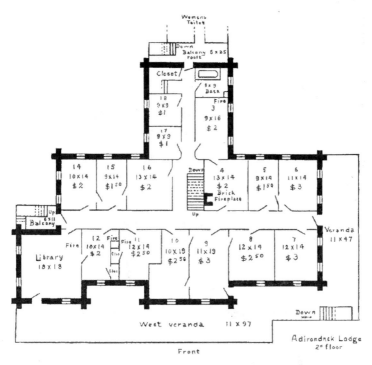

In 1877 a party of New Yorkers, mountain enthusiasts, drew plans for an ideal forest home to be known as Adirondack Lodge. After studying the maps they chose from the highest peak in the state, Tahawus, the best square mile in all the great forest in which to "get nearest to nature's heart." Having found the owners 640 acres were bought and in 1878 the Lodge was built of huge spruce logs. It has since been the most famous building in the Adirondacks. Later changes of management and lack of capital prevented needed improvements, to the great regret of many admirers of the wonderful location.

The entire plant was bought October 1900 for Lake Placid Club. The builder of the Lodge with a force of men spent the winter in needed restorations and renovations and it will open July 1, 1901, with the same supervision and high standards as the club. New equipment, boats, livery, furniture, linen and china supplement the renovation of the building. Clubhouse and Lodge are connected by telefone and telegraf and 1 or more trips with mail and supplies will be made daily each way by club carriages. Long distance telefone connects with all points.

As much of the charm of this forest life often consists in living in some favorit nook personally selected, the club keeps the materials on hand and on a day's notice can erect and furnish a tent on any site approved by the superintendent. These tents or outside rooms are 50c, $1 and $1.50 a day according to size. This allows many who could not endure the usual hardships and meager fare to enjoy the quiet of an isolated forest camp and yet have the best beds and table and many home comforts. Circular L gives full information about the Lodge and its surroundings, walks, drives, climbs, etc.

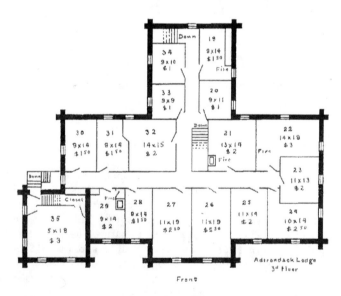

Front

There are also numerous rooms in lodges, cottages and tents at 50c, $1 and $1.50 a day according to size and location. New lodges or tents will be provided on a week's notice on any approved site selected by the occupant.

Lake Placid Club   Adirondack   Lodge   from southwest   1095

Club specialties

Housekeeping For those who prefer the greater independence, seclusion or economy of full or partial housekeeping there are 10 houses completely equipt with china, glass, silver, table and bed linen and cooking utensils so that nothing whatever need be brought or bought. The 5 houses markt *H* in House list are distant from club dining room and are for housekeeping only. The 5 markt *h* are within 3 minutes walk of the dining room and may be used either way. Some prefer to get their own breakfasts or teas or both, coming to the club only for dinners. Single dinners are 75c, other meals 50c Rent includes right to get at estimated cost any needed supplies, cookt or uncookt, from the club kitchen, cooler and storerooms. Cottages with facilities for partial housekeeping are Garden, Hillside, Nook, Orchard, Outlook and Woodside. The club also has several other houses in the village available for housekeeping. Rent of any house with care is the same as with housekeeping equipment without care and covers not only keeping the rooms in order, but also fuel, lights and laundry of house linen

Suites. A club specialty is suites, to give much of the conveniences and seclusion of a separate house with less care and cost. Many of these are engaged for a series of years and the occupants leave their mountain suits and various belongings exactly as they would in a private cottage. Suites can be made in scores of places by cutting off ends of corridors or combining adjoining rooms, while others are so connected that they are not rented as separate rooms. The following, with price a day without meals, are specially desirable. Those in italics can not be broken; others may be divided as wisht   Bath given with suites means private bath   Other suites all have the use of a bath near, often adjoining, and if the suite includes all rooms for which that bath was provided it becomes private without charge. Baths are public unless markt $1 on floor plans If exactly what is wanted is not found in this list, reference to floor plans will show that 1 or more adjoining rooms can be added to nearly every suite, thus enlarging it to fit the party

Lake Placid Club house   from south

Suite list

Suites in italics can not be broken, others may be divided as wisht
See House list, p. 108, for abbreviations

1 **room and bath.** *Ch 27*, $2; *7G 14*, $2 50; *Ch 2*, $3; *Ch 37*, $3, *Ch 41*, $3; *7G 19*, $3, *Ch 1*, $4; *F 12*, $4; *7G 3*, $4; *7G 9*, $4; *Ch 3*, $5.

2 **rooms.** *Cl 5-6*, $1, Wb 3-4, $1; Wb 5-6, $1.50; *Bg 7-8*, $2; Or 3-4, $2; Or 10-11, $2; 7G 20-21, $2; Cl 1-2, $2.50; Ch 7-8, $2 50; F 10-11, $2.50; Gd 2-3, $2.50; 7G 4, 7, $2.50; 7G 5-6, $2 50; Ch 48-49. $3; Or 1-2, $3; Ng 9-10, $3 50; F 5, 8, $4; F 6-7, $4; Ch 11-12, $5; Ew 8-9, $5.

2 **rooms and bath.** Ch 26-27, 2.50; F 10-11, $3 50, 7G 14-15, $4; Ch 31-32, $5; Ch 54-55, $5; *F 2-3*, $5 50; Ch 37-38, $6; Gd 5-6, $7; Ch 3-4, $9; Gm 64-65, $9; Gm 74-75, $9.

3 **rooms.** Wb 2-4, $2; Wb 5-7, $2; Bg 6-8, $2 50; Cl 4-6, $2.50; Ng 12, 14, 15, $2 50; Or 1, 6, 7, $4; 7G 4, 7, 8, $4 50, Ng 6-8, $5.

3 **rooms and bath.** *Ch 56-58*, $5, Ch 25-27, $5.50; Ch 31-33, $6; 7G 17-19, $6, Ch 53-55, $6 50, *Ch 16-18*, $7; Ch 37-39, $7 50, Ch 3-5, $11; *Gm 61-63*, $11, *Gm 71-73*, $11

4 **rooms.** Wb 5-8, $2 50, Cl 3-6, $3; Bg 5-8, $3.50; Ew 1-4, $4; Wb 1-4, $4; Or 8-11, $5 50, Gd 7-10, $6; Ch 42-45, $8; F 5 8, $8; Ch 10-13, $9

4 **rooms and bath.** Ch 24-27, $6; Ch 56-59, $6, *Hs 6-9*, $6 50, 7G 12, 14-16, $7, Ch 52-55, $7.50, F 9-12, $7 50, Wi 4-7, $8; Wi 8-11, $8; Gm 64-67, $15; Gm 74-77, $15

5 **rooms.** Bg 5-9, $4; 7G 4-8, $7

5 **rooms and bath.** *Hs 1-5*, $7.50; Ch 51-55, $8, Gd 2-6, $11

6 **rooms** Cl 1-6, $5.50; Or 1-7, $7.

7 **rooms and bath.** Ch 41-47, $13

Rented only as a whole: Ba, Ca, Nk, Ol, P, PL, Ss, Wa, Wo and the houses for housekeeping only, Co, Eg, Eh, Hl, Th.

Nearly all 1st floor cottage rooms have outside entrances so they can be used independently of the rest of the house. Specially detacht rooms are: Ba 11, 12, 50c each; Ca $1: F4 $1; Gd 4 $1 : N Lh $2: Wa 4 $1

Lake Placid Club.   From Mirror Lake Inn beach

Furniture. No carpets are used except to deaden sound of footsteps in halls or on stairs Mattings have been put in a few rooms where floors proved unsatisfactory. All new rooms have hard finisht birch or maple floors laid in narrow strips or in patterns and supplied with rugs as more attractiv and sanitary than carpets

Fireplaces. The regular fireplace is 1.25 m (50 in.) wide, burning 1 m (40 in) wood For smaller rooms there are 1 m, 75 cm and for extreme cases 50 cm (40, 30 and 20 in.) fireplaces. Wood and kindling are kept cut for all sizes, in 30, 40, 50, 75, and 100 cm (12, 16, 20, 30, and 40 in) lengths.

Terms

Engaging rooms. The club is not for transients but is a summer home for families, open only to members and their guests Others may be admitted for a first visit only on introduction of 2 members or on references approved by the trustees Such guests may become associates for the current season by paying the $10 fee required of all members, and have the same privileges except the right to issue invitations and privilege cards   .

Rooms are not reservd for August unless as part of an engagement of 6 weeks or more. As there are never rooms enough in August positiv engagements for a week or 2 then would inevitably crowd out others wishing to stay longer and also leave the rooms vacant before and after, to the serious loss of the club. Definit rooms may be reservd for 4 weeks or more if wholly in the first or second half of the season; i. e. if the engagement ends by August 10, or begins not earlier than August 11. Rooms reservd for shorter periods are subject to change if necessary to accommodate those engaging for the season or completing suites, the member moved being provided with other satisfactory quarters The superintendent will take any amount of trouble to accommodate members as far as possible without injustice to others He can sometimes arrange dates of short engagements of 2 or more parties so that the required 5 or 6 weeks may be divided between them. Early application will greatly increase the chance of making such a combination of dates. Except in August, when every house is

Lake Placid Club   North end from west

497

full, members may engage accommodations for even a single day and a place will be saved somewhere, tho the exact room preferd may be then occupied   The club, unlike a hotel, must treat all exactly alike and all engagements must therefore conform to above rules

Prices. Meals and rooms are charged separately and cost together in midseason $14 to $52.50 a week; before July 10 and after September 10, $12.25 to $31.50.   If 2 or more occupy 1 room it greatly reduces cost as no charge is made for an extra bed except $1 a week for care and laundry.   Meals are at actual cost: $1.50 a day; children under 12 and maids $1 a day in east and center dining rooms.

Standard club rooms, B, are $1.50, $2 and $2.50 a day. Smaller, or C rooms, none of which have open fires or other extras, are 50c and $1 a day.   Choicest and largest, or A rooms, with private baths, open fires, desks, study lamps, easy chairs, couches, bookcases or other extras are $3, $4 and $5 a day.   Private baths are $1 a day.

Extras. The club aims to let every member have anything he wishes and will pay for if it interferes with no one else Obviously *carte blanche* to order extras without charge is impracticable   Extras are therefore rented so that each guest may feel entire freedom in asking for them, the returns all being used in keeping up the accommodation   The club keeps on hand and will sell or rent almost any article needed for comfort or convenience; e g folding beds, extension, reclining and other easy chairs, open and close stoves, desks, office tables, etc.   Weekly rent is about 5% of cost, e. g. a $10 easy chair would be 50c If the average time of renting was 4 weeks the 20% found necessary to cover wear, interest, insurance, storage and depreciation on such easily injured articles would thus be paid

Special suites   On the same principle private baths or special rooms, suites, lodges or cottages are each year built for members who have definit wishes to gratify.   The aim is to make a summer home where members can have just what they wish   The superintendent tries to grant every reasonable request if necessary cost is paid either directly or in increast rent.   This system, like dining *a la carte*, sometimes results in annoying trifling charges, but in no other way can the club provide equitably for all its members   Each feels free to

Lake Placid Club   Adirondack Lodge   Heart of the Adirondacks   1051

gratify his preference since he pays for what he has and so adds nothing to cooperativ living expenses of his fellow members.

Invariable prices. The common summer hotel practice of 'charging as much as the case will bear' is strictly forbidden. Every item of expense has its cost plainly printed and this can be changed no more than price of postage stamps. Each guest thus gets without 'bargaining' the most favorable terms obtainable.

Half rates. To induce visits out of the crowded season, rooms, private baths and boats are only half price before July 10 and after September 10.

Season. Midseason with full staff in all departments is from July 10 to September 10. The club is open June 1 to November 1, or 5 months each year, with as large a staff and such service as the number of members in residence warrants.

Postoffice address. June 1 to November 1 Lake Placid Club, Morningside, Essex co. N. Y.; rest of year, Asa O Gallup, Secretary, 15 W 43 st. New York.

Lake Placid Clubhouse   from northwest

Location of Lake Placid Club

NEW YORK CENTRAL
& HUDSON RIVER R. R.
ADIRONDACK MOUNTAINS
AND MONTREAL LINES.

Lake Placid Club Morningside N.Y.

North end of Mirror lake section

K H G F E D C B A

NORTHWOOD

BEECHWOOD

Woodside Lodge

North lake house

Northgate

Hillside

North lake house

Sentinel lake house

Orchard

Beechwood road

Water Tower

Boat house

Edgewater

Barn
Ice

Garden

Balsams

Tennis

Uplands road

Children's dock

Rogue

LAKESIDE

Swimming school

Clubhouse

Maidery

Pines

Lake library

Maidery

Bath cabins

Cooler

Canoehouse

Lake house

Winona

Boat house

Gambrels

Cabin

Boat house

Sunnyside

Pine

Nook

Seven Gables

Tennis

Boathouse

Baygrove

Outlook

BROOKWOOD

Wayside

Station

Boat house

Forest

Brookwood spring

Woodbine

Forest Courts

Clematis

Maidery

LAKEWOOD

VALLEY FARM

Edgewood road

Base ball and cricket grounds

St Armand hole

Short Links

Stables

Carriage roads ====
Paths and trails ——

Each block is 40 meters or 8 rods square

MIRROR LAKE

HILLCREST

Valley road

Garden road

Houses with *h* prefixt can be had at same rent completely equipt for housekeeping; *H* means for housekeeping only as they are too far from club dining room to go for meals.

House	Abbreviation	From Clubhouse		Living rooms	Baths	Toilets	Water faucets		Fires		Price a day
		Direction	Feet				Cold	Hot	Open	Stoves	
Adirondack Lodge	L	s.	10m.	60	1	6E	17	6	5	6	
h Balsams	Ba	e.	850	12	1	2	4	4	2	2	$10 50
Baygrove	Bg	s.	425	9		1	2			2	7
Cabin	Ca	e.	630	1							1
h Clematis	Cl	s.	1085	6		1A	1		1	1	5 50
Clubhouse	Ch			90	16	28	69	76	25	6*	
H Colden	Co	s.e.	½m.	6						3	?4
H Eastgate	Eg	s e.	½m.	6						3	?4
H Edgehill	Eh	s.w.	2m.	12		2E				5	?6
Edgewater	E w	n.	385	9	1	1	5		3	2	12 25
Forest	F	s.	748	18	4	4	10	10	3	9C	22
Gambrels	Gm	s.	15	20	4	6	17	15	6	34R	
Garden	Gd	n.	212	11	2	2	6	5	2	4C	17
H Highland	Hl	s. w	2½m.	?10			1				?4
Hillside	Hs	n.	650	9	2	2	6	5	4	2C	14
Nook	Nk	s.e.	500	9	1	2	4	3	3	2C	12
h Northgate	Ng	n.	712	13	1	2	4	3	3	7	17
North lakehouse	NLh	n.	770	1		1A				1	2
Orchard	Or	n.	550	11	1	1	4	3	1	2C	12 50
Outlook	Ol	s.e.	620	8	1	2	9	8	1	5C	12
h Pines	P	e.	503	10	1	2	9	7	4	2	12 50
Pine lodge	PL	s.e.	437	2		1	2		1		3 50
Seven Gables	7G	s.	270	18	5	5	13	12	5	7C	
Sunnyside	Ss	s.e.	325	9	1	2	4	5	2	2C	12 50
H Theanoguen	Th	s.e.	½m.	12							
Wayside	Wa	s.	600	7	1	1	4	3	1	2	8
Westside	We	w.	⅓m.	4		1	2		2	1	5
Winona	Wi	e.	100	11	2	2	5	5	4	1C	17 50
h Woodbine	Wb	s.	1040	8	1	1	2	2	1	2	6 50
Woodside Lodge	Wo	n.	820	4	1	1	3	4	1	2C	7
Total				406	46	79	203	176	80	215	
Tents											
Cabin	CaT	e.	640								1
Cherries	CsT	e.	400	5							2
Idlewild	I T	s.e.	400								1 50
Pavilion	Pa T	e.	80								1 50
St Armand	St A T	e.	80								1 50
Seven Gables	7G T	s e.	100								1 50
Sunnyside	Ss T	s.e.	100								1 50
Winona	Wi T	s.e.	100								1 50
Waneka	Wk T	s.e.	400								1 50

A—in annex; C—coal heater; E—earth closet; *h*—equipt for housekeeping; *H*—for housekeeping only; R—radiators. *Also 100 radiators.

Lake Placid Club
Morningside N Y

Report and announcement to members 1901

Unusually full announcements for 1900 will be found on p 37-52 of Handbook   These notes are merely of additions and improvements for 1901.   The circulars and handbooks should be consulted for a statement of what the club offers under each head, specially the new circulars on amusements and on Adirondack Lodge.   Prices, rules and general plan remain the same as in 1900   Changes are simply the natural evolution of original ideas with elimination each year of what has been found undesirable, retention of what has been most appreciated and approved and improvement wherever practicable.

The last year was markt by larger additions and more rapid development than any 2 years since the club started   In buildings, grounds and plant the year was most satisfactory, but in service, table and laundry we were so far short of the standards set that a complete reorganization has been made for 1901   Mr Asa O Gallup, president of the N. Y. preparatory school, 1 of the 3 original founders of the club, will give his entire summer as superintendent, and having studied the problem all last summer, assures us with confidence that the matters justly criticized in 1900 will be satisfactory for 1901.   To insure this over $5000 more than heretofore has been placed at his disposal for necessary improvements of service, table and laundry   The trustees will have nothing whatever to do with the administration of the club except as they may vote on needed rules or take necessary action as a board, having transferd to Mr Gallup all authority and made him sole administrativ officer.   He has accepted this responsibility and those who know his reputation and experience as an executiv officer have entire confidence that this department will hereafter be as satisfactory as the unrivaled location and plant.   Our growth has made it possible to assign to table and service a larger sum than ever before because greatly increast numbers reduce pro rata the fixt charges.   But this same growth was responsible for serious deficiences in the organization of last year.   The 4 new officers, steward, chef, head waiter and head laundress will be experienced specialists who have dealt with larger numbers than ours, so

Cr30N33Mr1

that we can rely on prompt and efficient kitchen, table and laundry service and the removal of those difficulties which arose from a growth beyond the capacity of the plant or the ability of some of the staff to handle properly

New buildings. For the use of our help we have completed during the winter 2 large buildings with rooms and baths, 1 with complete home equipment, thus relieving the kitchen and adding greatly to its efficiency and convenience. Experience having shown the impossibility, with mountain difficulties, of relying on promises to finish buildings on time, this work was done last fall and winter so that early comers this year will be free from noise and confusion of building. Since the last announcement there have been completed Outlook and Hillside, 2 of our best cottages, and the Nook near Pine lodge will soon be done. The new Menery for the male help was finisht in December and in March the best stable and carriage-house yet built in this region. A dry kiln holding 50,000 ft of lumber, and a tool house have been added in Valley Forge The golf library and the canoe house and lake library were finisht last fall 30 men and 16 horses were employd most of the winter on the estate. An outlook tower on the summit of Hill-crest has comfortable stairs to the highest viewpoint of the vicinity, the picturesque construction covering a high service fire protection tank holding 50,000 gallons of water with 120 ft head

Housekeeping. 4 new houses will be ready for complete housekeeping this season Edgehill is our best farm house, 2 miles to the west, price $300 · . Theanoguen has been improved by adding running water and complete plumbing. There is an excellent stable and servants house, and added furnishing will be provided with whatever else is necessary to make it the best of the club houses and to maintain its reputation as the best estate in the vicinity. It stands on the eastern edge of the golf links a half mile from Clubhouse, on the great rock on the summit of the 16 acres, largely forest, known as Knollwood The house was built by the family of Bishop Henry C. Potter of New York, and in years when they were absent it has been occupied by J Pierpont Morgan and others who have wisht the most desirable house in the Placid region. Parlor 30x18, dining room 18x15, kitchen 16x11, shed 14x6, pantry 11x7, piazza

30x9, coverd balcony on 2d floor, 14 bedrooms; price, as in the past before recent improvements were made, $1200.

Estate. Northwood, adjoining Woodside and Northgate, has been bought, also Theanoguen and Knollwood, 16 acres

The great addition of the year is the 640 acres and 16 buildings of the famous Adirondack Lodge property, which will open July 1 as the forest branch of the club. Details of this are given in the special illustrated Lodge circular.

A half dozen minor purchases of land have been made at points where desirable for protection or future development. Several more old buildings have been demolisht, making a total of 69 torn down in the 5 years work of improvement.

Farms. The old Elba house farm has been bought and added to Highland and Edgehill, the 3 joining and giving us a great club farm of 500 acres with all necessary buildings and other equipment   Important additions and repairs have been made to barns and stables and new milk and ice house and cooler built at Highland. 20 cows carefully selected by an expert will be added to the club herd this spring. A specially successful farmer has been secured to give his entire time to the club farms, which will be steadily improved from year to year as fast as practicable without extravagance.

Maple sugar. For the same reason that we raise our own milk, the club forester is making this year from the famous orchard at Adirondack Lodge a supply of maple sugar and syrup for club use   We shall have the best and know that every practicable precaution has been taken to insure absolute cleanliness in all the processes.

Brookwood spring. This remarkably fine spring is within 5 minutes walk of the club and furnishes the purest water in abundance for the club tables, where it is used exclusivly.

Improvements. A new road via Greenacre improves the station drive and a new trail has been made from Forest courts to golf houses   Several thousand dollars have been spent in better water supply and extra fire protection. This was examind by the insurance board, which reported that no other Adirondack plant had protection nearly as thoro as was afforded by changes in construction, our 120 ft head with 12 standpipes and hose lines inside and hydrants outside the building, with a plentiful supply of chemical and other extinguishers, and 200

firepails and other appliances We have our own plumbing
shop, thus giving better work, closer supervision and prompter
repairs than would be otherwise possible The shop has util-
ized the winter by adding several new baths and making the
former plant still better   We now have 46 baths, 78 lavatories
and 79 toilets. There are 176 hot and 203 cold running water
faucets. Both Clubhouse and Lodge have long distance telefones to all points.

Constant additions are made to insure comfort, specially
on the chilly days and nights inevitable in the mountains, there
being over 100 hot water radiators, 80 open and 81 other fires
Scores of people familiar with the best Adirondack hotels have
inspected the club plant and have without exception declared it
far in advance of any other in conveniences and protection
against possible accidents and injury to health In mere fashion
and display it will always be far behind, but will hold first place
in those things which it has esteemd worthy its special attention. Additions this year are · running hot water at Wayside,
Woodbine, Orchard, Woodside, Hillside, Menery and Maidery;
near front stairs of Clubhouse, 2d floor, a central hot water
room with solid porcelain slop sinks and equipment, duplicating
that so much liked in Gambrels; in the basement a public bath
and shower bath.

The most prominent feature of the year has been the rapid
completion of the plant for doing all our own work. The lumber grows on club land, is cut by our men, drawn by our own
teams to our own mill where it is sawd and workt, and experience has proved that our 10 shops do everything better than we
could otherwise get it done and at less cost. This gain has
made it possible to release just so much more money for current
running expenses and so give better accommodations and service without increase of price. The new steam mill and shops
have been built opposit the railroad station in order to take the
noise and confusion a mile from Clubhouse, as well as to save
expense by having the club lumber yard on the railroad siding
where heavy freight can be placed in the storehouses directly
from the cars without use of teams

Golf. The telefone line crossing the links has been moved.
The new work agreed on by the golf committee as most desirable has been done at large cost and the links will be much

better than ever. The golf library, with ladies room and kitchen, caddies stand, and a liberal supply of benches at various points, adds to the attractions of our unrivald links The 5 o'clock teas will be maintaind weekly and it is intended this year to add music. Members will be free to invite friends from the hotels and cottages, thus making it a delightful out-of-doors feature. Simple refreshments will also be available thru the week at the golf houses.

Boating. A boat house for the Forest group of cottages has been provided and our boat shop has workt all winter on new boats, still farther improving our fleet, already well known as the best in the mountains. Canoeing is increasing yearly and will be farther encouraged. Rev W. W. Moir, as chairman of the general Adirondack regatta committee, is already planning for the summer's races, which are to be held on the club courses. Prof. Ernest Allen will this year have immediate charge of the lake front as well as of the swimming school, and will arrange for the club and house regattas and other lake entertainments.

A cycle repairer will be on duty at the lakehouse to clean and care for wheels.

Swimming school. The club is fortunate in having secured the services for the entire season of the most famous teachers of scientific swimming in this country, Prof. Ernest Allen and his wife. Needed facilities have been added, swimming trolley, diving pedestal, 30 bath cabins, 400 ft of board walk, so that with best teachers, best water and best conveniences the club's first rank as a swimming center will be unquestiond. Prof. Allen has repeatedly proved his ability to make expert swimmers out of old and young who had thought they could not learn, and those who met him last summer will give him a cordial welcome on his return.

Driving The new club stable is the best in the region 12 new carriages will be deliverd in June, and with new harnesses and horses the club livery will hereafter be a specialty just as boating and golf have been heretofore. The new equipment, supplementing the best of that bought last year, will make the stable a markt feature both at the club and at the Lodge. There will be offerd this year facilities impracticable in a public hotel but very desirable for club members they give it more the character of a private estate

Climbing. Adirondack Lodge with 50 miles of trails thru the forest to the finest scenery of eastern America has been known for 20 years as the best point of the Adirondacks for camping parties and mountain climbing. This will be made one of the club's great specialties hereafter. Mr. Henry van Hoevenberg, who built the Lodge, has been made club forester and will be in residence to afford any needed assistance to club members young or old. A carriage will run regularly each way between club and Lodge, materially reducing labor and expense of making these most famous excursions, and opening the way for more outdoor life in the "Heart of the Adirondacks" At the Lodge the traditional Wednesday night camp fire and stories, and at the club the cathedral and lake fires which have been a feature from the beginning, will be kept up.

Forest courts. The valley to the north has been fild, making room for the entire 8 courts as pland, and new ones will be added as needed   3 more will be available this year than last so there will be ample facilities for all outdoor games requiring courts

Music. Last year the music committee tried 4 different orchestras and were unanimous as to the best. This has been secured for 3 or 4 times a week during the entire season. Instead of 1 annual german and 1 float night and general illumination of the lake each will occur monthly, about July 20, August 15 and September 10. The traditional "Sunday night sing" will be continued and there will be weekly concert programs besides 2 evenings for dancing   With the new grand piano, 1901 will mark a distinct advance in both quality and quantity of good music.

Library. This will be much larger than that so much used last year and will soon number 2000 volumes. To encourage members interested to study club specialties more thoroly libraries are being developt on golf, boating, driving, mountain climbing, camping, forestry, outdoor and indoor sports and allied subjects. Members interested in carrying on the plans for the museum, zoo, botanic garden, aquarium, etc (see p 42 of Handbook) are requested to send notice of the subjects in which they are willing to cooperate. We have now provided rooms and needed facilities and can give garden space and necessary help, and these features can be developt as fast as members interested will do their part.

Kindergarten. A good start was made last year by the 2 traind kindergartners, who took the little children 5 mornings a week for nature study and suitable games This will be made a regular feature.

Traind nurses. Besides a city physician, there will be in residence 1 or more traind nurses in readiness for any emergency

New publications. The long delayd Handbook is now being bound and will be maild to members early in April This gives the fullest information, is completely indext, is bound conveniently for preservation in the library, and should be put in the hands of those enough interested to preserve it Extra copies can be had at 25c

Other publications of interest to members are: map of grounds showing location of all cottages, circular on amusements showing the club's unusual facilities, with list of drives, walks, available games, etc

Photografy. A "dark room" with all conveniences will be provided at Clubhouse in addition to that heretofore used in Westside lakehouse.

Photografs Scores of new pictures better than any before obtaind were made during the year and have been added to the club albums. Copies can be had at the office and members ordering 5 or more are furnisht free with binding covers so that the collection can be kept on an ordinary book shelf Several of the finest views have been made in paper weights at 25c each; also in larger form suitable for framing. The artistic merit of these wall pictures is recognized by all experts in modern photografy.

Half tones. Half tones on cards 12½x20 cm with rings for hanging on the wall, have also been made thus giving inexpensiv but excellent pictures of our best scenery. There is also a 16 page pamflet of new half tone pictures, as well as private mailing cards with Inn beach view of Clubhouse and grounds, at 50c a 100.

Calendars and blotters. These are printed twice a year in postal and note size and may be had free or will be maild to addresses sent in They reproduce in half tone some of the best views of the club and its surroundings

Oil sketches. Mr J. C Nicoll N A whose pictures at
the Columbian exposition, at Paris and elsewhere have won him
so much credit for American landscapes, has made a series of
studies in the immediate vicinity of the club, most of them on
its grounds It is so desirable that these should be ownd by
those who not only appreciate them as pictures but who also
know and love the place, that the collection has been bought
and given to the club to be sold to its members and guests, the
entire proceeds being used for additions to the club library

Engagement of rooms. Each year some are disappointed
because they neglect to engage their rooms till so late that
nothing entirely satisfactory can be found. The superintendent
is responsible for making both ends meet in club running
expenses and therefore must engage rooms to those who apply
earliest if they are members or associates or hold privilege cards.

Finances. The most gratifying item of the annual report
is that club growth has made it possible to readjust agreements
so that without any increase of prices a larger sum than ever
before will be available for cooperativ expenses of maintenance.

The club gains by this reorganization of business interests
just completed With working capital more than doubled,
expenses can be reduced and profits to others cut off in various
directions The heavy fixt charges for maintaining the great
estate, while larger in total each year, arc less a burden because
divided among so many more members and guests. The new
agreement between the corporation owning the plant, and the
superintendent and council representing the club members
is the same as before. except:

1 The entire fees of members, which went to maintain
grounds, will be spent directly for club purposes, the company
assuming all expenses to which fees have been heretofore
applied

2 All profits from the boat liveries, which increase each
year, go to the club instead of to the company, while the farms,
which tho giving much better milk and vegetables have shown
a loss, are transferd from club to company

3 Mr Barnett's club livery was bought and greatly improved so that with resulting larger patronage it now shows a
profit. This also is given wholly to the club which thus has for
paying its expenses all profits from boating, driving, golf, bowl-

ing, billiards, pool and all forms of amusements as well as from
table and laundry.

4 Various items such as fuel, lights, water, depreciation
of furniture and equipment, flat laundry work and superintendent's salary properly payable as current club expenses, have for
the present been assumed by the company, thus releasing a
large sum yearly for improving table and service which can
thus be made distinctly better.

As from the first organization of the club, the plan remains
that members who furnish working capital as preferd stock are
to have 6% interest   For $1000 or more, there is exemption from
annual club dues of $10, thus making the highest possible
return 7%   The bonds for $100,000 issued April 1, 1891, at 5%,
refund the floating debts at a saving of $1000 a year.   The
holders of the common stock of $100,000 agree to provide for
club use the completely equipt plant as in the past with the
material concessions named above, to furnish necessary capital,
to pay 5% on the bonds and 6% on preferd stock, and to guaran-
tee all debts and bills of the club, provided the superintendent elected by the council shall be approved by the trustees,
who retain the right to make any rules to protect against loss,
waste or extravagance

In this revised and enlarged organization the club thus con-
tinues on the original plan of 1895, modified only in minor
details which insure to members even more satisfactory accommodations and service than in the past.   The plan as revised
and now in effect reads as follows:

Method and effect of cooperation   All receipts from
table, kitchen, service, laundries, liveries, excursions, entertainments, golf, athletics, boating, bowling, billiards and other
amusements, telegraf, telefones, postoffice, barber shop,
etc. are spent by the superintendent solely to give the most
possible to members.   No one can financially profit by them.
The larger they can be made each year the better the club will
be for that year.   Members furnish no capital and assume no
risks of deficits.   They pay a fixt price, only enough to cover
actual cost of maintenance and reasonable rent for the completely furnisht plant built and maintaind for this special use
The Lake Placid Co is a corporation composed wholly of club
members who own this plant and furnish needed capital and
assume all risks and responsibilities and accept the rent receivd

in full for insurance, taxes, depreciations, repairs, expenses and interest on their investment. Members thus get the benefit of pure cooperation without the financial risks inevitable if they ownd the costly plant, or the indefinitness if cost were not decided till the season's accounts were balanced Thru the advice of the council of representative members, standards and methods are made what the club as a whole prefers in its summer home.

Club accounts are in 30 distinct divisions, each kept as strictly as if for a critical individual owner who would scrutinize each charge The month's footings enable the council and trustees to see exactly how club income is spent and where greater economy or change of price is needed or where more liberality may safely be allowd The indefinitness of estimates or loosely kept accounts is thus avoided and best possible returns for money spent are made possible

Club bonds. The most important subject of the year is the issue April 1, 1901, of $100,000 gold coupon bonds bearing semiannual interest at 5%. In order to issue these, other mortgages were paid in full, thus giving perfect titles and making the bonds absolutely first mortgage on 1986 acres of land and 49 buildings, besides the entire personal property and franchises. The bond circular gives full details. Every member who can do so conveniently is urged to cooperate in the development of the club at the same time that he makes an unusually safe and desirable investment for himself by helping furnish capital Each member who holds $1000 bonds at 5% or preferd stock at 6% is a life member, exempt from annual dues, so that he really gets the best of security and (counting dues saved) 6% or 7% interest. He also has certain extra privileges in engaging rooms and introducing friends. Under the preceding arrangement life members contributed $1000 each and had no formal or legal security for their principal Now that the mortgages have been paid off there is more than double security so that financial experts who have lookt the matter over carefully pronounce the investment unusually safe and desirable.

These bonds have been made specially for members and not for sale to the public. It is believd that every member who holds club securities thereby becomes more interested in its welfare, and the trustees therefore wish to have every member make such investment in its working capital as is convenient, but as in the past, this is wholly optional

Membership

This circular explains eligibility, rights, privileges and responsibilities of the various forms of membership

The club is not open to the public and so does not advertise. It depends for any desired increase in numbers solely on personal invitations extended by present members to those who they believe will add personally to the attractions of the summer home at Morningside.

The club's object is by cooperation to secure among congenial people and beautiful natural surroundings the privileges of an ideal summer home, with the highest standards of health, comfort and convenience, quiet and rest, and attractiv amusements and recreations.

Introductions. Invitations to a first visit may be issued on any member's recommendation by a privilege card good for 2 weeks, without payment of any fee   Invited friends may make a longer stay by becoming associates, as explaind below.

Associates. Those who after a first visit find the club congenial and like its plans and standards may, on invitation, become associates on payment of the annual fee of $10, due May 1 or whenever rooms are engaged for the year.   This entitles them to the same prices and discounts as full members and to all club privileges except voting and issuing privilege cards or invitations, which must be signd by a regular member or trustee   This is the usual form of membership and is preferd by all who wish to enjoy club privileges with the least possible responsibility.

Members. None are invited to full membership till they have spent sufficient time at the club as associates or guests to know that they are in cordial sympathy with its aims and methods and are willing to cooperate in advancing its best interests.   Election must be by unanimous vote   Members may reserve rooms in advance and issue privilege cards good for 2 weeks to any friends for whom they assume full responsibility as being satisfactory club guests   They alone are eligible for life membership or to serve on the council or any committee and may recommend to the council or trustees such changes and improvements as they believe for the best interests of the club. By taking bonds or preferd stock, or lending funds to cover cost of building and furniture they may have special cottages built for them on selected sites and may hold a lease for a term of years, or without lease may have first choice in occupying a special cottage each year, having no ownership or responsibility in case they wish to go abroad or for any reason desire to resign their membership. They have no responsibility of management and no liability for expenses except the annual fee of $10.

As their election is thus only to the social and cooperativ privileges of the club they have no legal right to modify by direct vote its organization, management or policy, such responsibilities and powers being limited by constitution to life members, who own the entire club property. The members, however, secure their preferences by electing a council to which the trustees refer all questions which in their nature should be decided by the members of the club rather than by the owners of the plant.

. **Life members.** Any member who contributes $1000 or more to the working capital of the club, either by loan or by taking preferd stock at 6% or gold coupon bonds at 5% semiannual interest, becomes a life member and is exempt from the annual $10 dues. He may be elected a trustee and has the right because of financial interests to vote on all questions of policy and administration, including the annual election of trustees.

Honorary members. By unanimous vote the trustees may invite to honorary membership persons who by their knowledge of arts and sciences represented in the club's development or by their interest and sympathy with its ideals can render valuable assistance by keeping in touch with its progress and from time to time giving their advice. Honorary members can often make only occasional short visits but they are kept on the permanent roll without payment of annual fee, their introductions of friends are honord and they are always welcome when rooms are available.

Council. This consists of members appointed by the trustees from nominations by the club To it are referd questions involving social privileges of members, invitations, amusements, entertainments, house rules, ethical standards and such other matters as are chiefly determined by personal preferences and so should be decided by the members in residence and not by the owners of the plant.

The council or trustees may terminate any membership by unanimous vote if at any time the club's best interests should require it   In such cases any investment in club property must be returnd to the member.

Organization.   The club is not like most American clubs, ownd equally by its members and administerd by a committee appointed by them.   It is organized like the clubs so common in England, on the plan adopted also for some in America, e. g. the Albany country club.   A company of friends wish a large country estate for common use and are willing to pay running expenses and interest on necessary investment but not to furnish needed capital to buy outright a costly plant.   A few enthusiasts in such cases furnish the capital in order to make the club possible and take the risk of its financial ability to pay rent or interest agreed on   Socially it is like other clubs, in its control of its membership and guests, and its recreations and club life and in sharing necessary expenses, including pro rata rent of plant, instead of paying extravagant profits to a hotel   But legally it is a proprietary club, free from the financial responsibilities of ordinary clubs

Obviously only life members who have contributed to needed capital and are incorporated as the Lake Placid Co. share in ownership and business control.   The regular members and associates contribute no capital and are free from all legal, moral or financial responsibilities beyond personal bills and annual $10 fee.   No person can engage rooms at the club or enjoy its privileges unless he pays this fee as a member or an associate or is temporarily the guest of some member.   There is no other way of coming to the club, for it is not a hotel.   All persons at the club must therefore be either members or associates, or their guests.   The organization has been carefully framed under legal advice, to guard against any possible entanglement by which members or associates could become in the slightest degree personally responsible for the financial management of the club.

Introductions

The Lake Placid club often has inquiries from persons whose names are not on its books and who mention no member as introducing them   Some have been invited to the club by a

member who has neglected to send their names to the secretary.
Some have not understood that the club is open only to its
members and their guests and to those specially invited by the
trustees after satisfactory introductions. In all cases we send
the information askt with this explanatory statement and an
outline of the club's distinctiv features. In some cases full
understanding of just what the club is removes any desire to
visit it, and correspondence can be dropt. If however this
farther knowledge creates a decided interest and wish to know
the club, it should be rememberd that those most attracted by
its peculiar plan are the very ones most likely to be welcomd
as visitors, and later as permanent members   Obviously its
chief safeguard and charm are based on the invariable rule
that a satisfactory introduction must precede the first visit.

Those wishing an invitation to the club should refer to
several persons of the class likely to be members or well known
to some members   These are clergymen, literary men, librarians and chiefly college and university officers or graduates
The club is often called the Wilderness university club, tho in
fact college graduation has nothing to do with admission. All
its founders chanced to be activ in university, college and
library work   It has grown from personal invitations without
advertising, and naturally the friends of these members came
largely from the same class.   This has brought together an
unusually cultivated circle, so that many have assumed from the
obvious high educational average that only college graduates
were eligible. We have however always much preferd an agreeable man who never saw a college to a university honor man
who was selfish, conceited or otherwise less clubable   The
real question about new members is whether they would appreciate and enjoy and be enjoyd by this particular club, which
differs so widely from a hotel   The club is glad to welcome
cordially such additions.

The following circular letter is sent to secure information for the guidance of the
committee which admits associates and guests

The trustees have been referd to you as being well
acquainted with M
of   who has
been proposed as an associate in this club   The inclosed circu-

lars will explain the club's peculiar character and you will see the kind of people who would be welcome additions and who would in turn enjoy club life much better than any possible hotel

The success of the club has been phenomenal It has grown tenfold in 5 years Its chief concern is to admit to full membership only those who believe cordially in its distinctiv features and it excludes religiously every person against whom there is social, race, moral or physical objection. No consumptiv is ever allowd to spend a night in a club room. This physical rule does not bar out convalescents or even invalids who, because of themselves or their families, are otherwise desirable additions, except in cases where there is possible danger to others or where the disease is annoying or a strain on the sympathies.

The club is liked best by cultivated people who wish all the comforts and conveniences of their own homes while enjoying the health-giving outdoor life of this wonderful climate and the inspiration of the magnificent mountain, lake and forest scenery. It is no place for mere fashion and display.

Will you kindly tell us in strict confidence if the name proposed is one that ought to be accepted in a club with our distinctiv features. In your judgment would it be agreeable to both the club and the member proposed? An early reply in the stampt envelop inclosed will be esteemed a favor

Should you be interested to know more of the club we will gladly send you any of its publications

Early and late visits

Numerous members and guests who would be very cordially welcomd at the club are disappointed every year because they can not get rooms Families leaving in early September to get home for schools relieve the pressure, and probably from then till the club closes, 6 or 8 weeks later, desirable rooms may be had.

June is here the rarest month of all the year but few enjoy it because of school or business engagements. Those who do come are enthusiastic. There is ample choice of rooms and a delightful sense of oceans of space everywhere

The same is true in the early fall September and October days make July and August seem tame. The splendor of the

brilliant autumn foliage with its bright reds and greens and
the marvelous clearness of the cooler air, which is like wine in
its tonic effects, always create the greatest enthusiasm among
those able to be here at that time. Now that over 100 hot water
radiators have been added to our 80 open and 81 other fires the
coolness of the longer evenings is a positiv attraction Happy
parties cluster around great fires of blazing logs, and halls,
baths and bedrooms are thoroly comfortable night and day

In spite of these greater attractions most people are forced
to take their vacation in July or August, when every room is
in demand. To induce those who can control their time to
select the preferable earlier and later dates all rooms, baths and
boats will be charged at only half price before July 10 and after
September 10. An increasing number are adopting the plan
of coming for a few days in the early season and again for a
fall visit in October, tho they take their regular vacation in July
and August. For house parties the early and late dates have
obvious great advantages because just the accommodations
wanted can so seldom be had in midseason.

The N. Y. C. sells, usually till October 31, round trip
tickets for 1 fare to Saranac lake, good for 15 days from date of
sale The club sends its half fare milage books between Saranac
and Placid, thus making the entire trip half fare. So low a
rate has never before been offerd, and many club members and
friends will improve the opportunity to get a few at least of the
incomparable October days, much the finest of the whole year
at Placid, when good rooms in either Clubhouse or cottages,
bath suites and boats are surely available and at half price
Golfers and other lovers of nature will find these the most
attractiv days of all the year.

Adirondack Lodge, put in thoro repair, is now the forest
branch of the club. This new and great addition with its 50
miles of trails direct to the most famous scenery in eastern
America, will lead to the formation of numerous parties for
climbing the mountains or going thru Indian and Avalanche
passes with the Lodge as headquarters

The club opens earlier and closes later, with more in residence, than any other Adirondack resort Its members wish to
be able to visit it any time from May 1 to November 1 To
secure enough guests to justify thus doubling the usual season
the club has gone to large expense to provide unusual comforts
and attractions for early and late visits, which it makes its distinct specialty. The chief attraction at the club is the people.
No greater service can be done by any member than to invite
friends who will be a distinct addition to Morningside to come
and see what it really is This *early and late* circular should
be sent to remind them of the desirability of coming before
or after the crowded midseason.

Lake Placid Club
Morningside N.Y.

Amusements and environment

Members are constantly askt 'what is there to do at the club?' Good rooms and meals can be had at many resorts but there are few if any places where nature, skilful plans and work and liberal expenditure have combined to offer so many healthful and desirable recreations. The details of this circular will be burdensome to some. Others are glad of a check list of little things that tempt out of doors on long summer days if no more than mere mention of ordinary short walks that others have found attractiv. As outdoor life is the club specialty, the first notes are on the general location and the character of the great club estate on which members spend most of their summer days.

Tahawus   Colden   Algonquin   Iroquois

CONTENTS

The summer problem has no greater difficulty for families than to find recreations which will strongly attract young and old, give new health and strength for the coming year's work, and be free from late hours and every flavor of physical or moral excess or dissipation. It is common experience that most people, who in theory fully believe in the great advantages of outdoor life and recreations, lack the initiativ to make use of them unless the way is made unusually easy and attractiv. A chief feature of the club is to induce practical recognition by its members that their mountain vacation is largely to get new health and strength from life with nature. It offers so many inducements to outdoor life in every practicable, health-giving form, that it is hard to resist the attractions, and young and old who have never done so before often enter heartily into it. The club begins by making this feature prominent in its printed matter, thus attracting as members those who already care most for nature, and so helping to increase the desirable nature-loving atmosphere. It then gives time and money liberally to developing and encouraging all that is best in out-door life.

Simplified spellings used are recommended by the English philological society and the American philological association including the leading language scholars of Oxford, Cambridge and the American universities, also by the latest and most authoritativ dictio   the Century and pr

As far as practicable amusements are all free. Concerts, amateur theatricals, lectures, stereopticon exhibitions and other entertainments in the theater or music room, pavilion or lakehouses, indoor or out, are free to all members and their guests without admission fee or collection, unless by special permission trustees have authorized a small charge or offering for some worthy charity or some unusual necessary expense of the entertainment. The ordinary hotel device of inviting to a free entertainment and then taking a collection for the benefit of the entertainers is not allowd. Where there is danger of monopoly of privileges by the thoughtless, or of other abuses, a charge is made, as for horses, boats, billiard and pool tables, and bowling alleys Pistol or rifle practice and glass ball shooting is allowd only at a distant point where the noise will not annoy cottagers, and careful protection is made against stray shots Courteous and experienced attendants are regularly provided at boat houses and alleys, but (except on request of those willing to pay the extra cost) not for games for which no charge is made, except as courts and grounds are put in good condition.

The following are free to all members and guests:

30 lockt bath cabins or dressing rooms with Turkish bath towels; 14 courts for tennis, croquet, roque, basket ball, quoits and other outdoor games needing level turf or dirt courts; 6-hole golf course of 1400 yards; baseball grounds; athletic field for cricket, hand ball, archery, bowls (English lawn) and similar games, or for field day, races, jumping and other outdoor sports; 3 shuffleboards, 4 swings, 4 see-saws and various other provisions for both old and young. Tennis courts at Pines, Garden and Theanoguen are for exclusiv use of those cottages.

. **Location.** This was chosen after 10 years search from 1883 to 1893, and no other spot has been found combining so many attractions. The best location in which to work out the ideal was persistently sought in visits extending from Nova Scotia to Mackinac and from Quebec to the Virginia and Tennessee mountains with special study of the Thousand Islands, the Catskills, Green and White mountains, and the Atlantic coast from Halifax to Cape May. Considering both natural beauty and healthfulness, the Adirondacks stood first, and Lake

Placid is by common consent most beautiful of the hundreds of resorts in the great forest. The cool nights and unusual freedom from Adirondack insect pests, with the wonderful tonic properties of its air, have given it world-wide fame as a haven for the tired and exhausted who wish to build up rapidly. Hay fever victims report it the safest refuge yet found. The lakes are 1863 ft above sea level, an ideal elevation which gives the tonic qualities without any of the disagreeable effects to sensitiv hearts felt at higher altitudes. It combines virgin forests with the most beautiful lakes, the highest and most numerous peaks and the most picturesque scenery. It is known as the driving center of the Adirondacks and the cycling maps show the roads to be the best in the mountains for wheelmen. A leading general guide book comparing this resort with others says: 'Lake Placid as a pleasure resort has a very select following and the best social elements have here full sway. It affords the nearest complete view of the most prominent peaks of the Adirondacks, likewise enchanting pictures of less elevated scenery. Its altitude, invigorating air and agreeable society make it one of America's most popular watering places.' A report to a national association by its president says after a summer spent at Placid:

The great forest or Adirondacks, the immense wilderness of northern New York, has long been famous, but comparativly few have seen more than the outskirts. When it took a week to journey in with guides and the cost of living was fourfold what is now charged for vastly better accommodations, it is not strange that few gave the necessary means and strength to the serious journey.

The new railway now brings you cheaply within a mile of peerless Placid, which all recognize as combining more attractions than any other place in this wonderful region An ideal summer home should have great mountains and the passes, cascades and other features that go only with them It should have abundant and beautiful waters for boating, fishing and bathing. It should have the great primeval forests about it. Many places have one, a few combine two of these essential elements, Placid has all three, each at its best.

The twin lakes, Mirror and Placid, recall to all traveld visitors the most beautiful of the Swiss and Scottish mountain lakes. The highest peaks of the state cluster about the plains of Placid like a coronet If a stranger were brought here blindfold and faced to the purest quarter of the circumference, he

would be satisfied the view deservd its fame till he had turnd
and found round the rest of the 360 degrees a still more beautiful mountain crown.   Within walking distance on all sides is
primeval forest which no ax has ever devastated.

The chief fame of the region is due to the marvelous effect
of the air.   Sick and well, weak and strong alike respond in a
single week to the health-giving qualities which have spread its
fame as wide as civilization.   Not only those with weak throat
or lungs, but all tired and overworkt, nervous, dyspeptic, and
indeed all who need a strong tonic without reaction find new
life and vigor here.   Few visitors can resist the temptation
to return year after year for their annual vacation, and to be
numberd among Placid enthusiasts, firm in the belief that here
is the earthly paradise.

Club estate.   During 8 years, 1893–1901, steady effort,
great care and liberal capital have been given to securing the
choicest locations in the acknowledgd choicest section of the
entire Adirondacks, the great forest recognized more widely
each year as unsurpast in all America as a summer home for
either health or natural beauties.   Over 80 pieces of real estate
have been combined in the club's 4000 acres of grounds, golf
links, forests, islands, fields and farms on Lakes Placid, Mirror
and Heart and on 5 rivers and numerous mountain brooks.   It
has many groves, woods and sugar orchards with scores of ideal
camp and picnic grounds.   Of the central section, Morningside,
the leading American authority on parks after detaild personal
inspection said: 'It is the most attractiv location for such a
private mountain park I have ever seen.   I doubt if another can
be found in America which combines in so small a space more
attractions of mountain views, lakes and forests.'   In most

cases the owners of property try to enhance its value by devising glowing theories about its remarkable advantages. These theories must therefore be taken with many grains of salt   In this case no member of the club had a dollar's previous interest in any of this property. Without prejudice in favor of any locality, long and careful study and comparison convinced the organizers that this was the best spot in the entire country for the purpose of this club   The property was therefore found and bought to fit the theory instead of making a theory to fit property in which the promoters were already financially interested.

The importance of our large area of choice forest will be understood by those who know that the state constitution of 1895 absolutely forbids any sale or lease or cutting of trees on the state lands which entirely surround this section.   While visitors may freely walk through the woods in all directions, they could not at any price secure the right to cut roads or paths, build camps, summer houses, outlooks and landings as may now be done on our 4000 acres   The organizers felt it important to secure ample forest land for such uses and spent much time in selecting and securing what study proved most desirable.

Over 80 separate purchases of land have been combined into a few principal sections, Morningside, Moose island, Overlook, West hights, Adirondack Lodge and the farms.   Morningside is the club home.   Its 5 chief divisions are Lakeside, about the central clubhouse; Lakewood including the forest coverd tract between the lake and the station road, Hillcrest, the summit east of Lakeside, Brookwood, the central forest from Forest courts to Bonniebrae and Valleyview on the east; and Mountain, the open highlands by the golf houses east of Lakewood.   In each of these sections there is to be built a central dining room for members who prefer these locations for their cottages or rooms.   The other sections in Morningside, which includes all east of the lake, are Uplands, the high land on the road from Hillcrest down to Meadowbrook; Whiteface slope, the field of evergreens at the entrance to Brookwood vista; Bonniebrae, the slopes at the south end of the vista running down to Meadowbrook; Valleyview, the summit on which stands Theanoguen overlooking the Plains of Abraham and the whole sweep into the mountains; Overbrook, the evergreen

Lake Placid Club Morningside N.Y.

North end of Mirror lake section

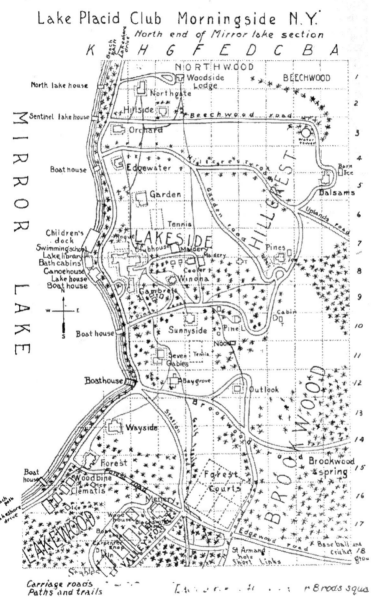

Carriage roads
Paths and trails

groves southeast of the golf links; the North or Meadowbrook farm extending to the river; the long and short golf links, formerly a part of this the oldest farm of the section; Greenacre, the grass coverd acre surrounded with every hue of forest green, thru the edge of which passes the station road; Midwood, between Greenacre and Forest courts; Valley Forge, the group of shops, stables, dry kiln and Menery, where all the club heavy work centers

Morningside woods and groves. There are within 15 minutes of Clubhouse, besides the fringe of trees along the lake front widening into Lakegrove at the 'quiet end,' 15 woods of 1 to 40 acres each, all on the club estate: Northwood and Beechwood, north of Hillcrest, are hardwood forest stretching north and east many miles before reaching any clearing; Pines grove or Hillcrest evergreens 1 a; Tamaracs, east of Uplands, 5 a; Winona wood, touching Clubhouse, 3 a. To the south in order are Fernwood pines 1 a; Wayside wood 5 a; Lakewood 40 a; Westwood, at foot of lake, 5 a; Midwood 5 a, Greenacre grove 2 a; Brookwood 40 a; including Bonniebrae 10 a; Valleyview and Theanoguen woods 10 a; Overbrook, south of golf links, 10 a. There are thus about a score of club woods and groves full of pretty nooks, glades and dingles for those who wish to get into the forest within a few steps of their rooms.

Equipment. On this broad foundation has been built a remarkable plant. Nothing has been done for fashion or display, but many thousand dollars have been spent in providing facilities for the most desirable recreations, which often contribute to the highest success of the summer outing as much as board and rooms together. This matter of wholesome amusements is made not a mere incident as is customary, but is studied, and time and money are given to it as freely as to what are called 'essentials,' like table, laundry and rooms The wide difference between the club and other resorts in this respect is felt more and more each year as plans are more fully carried out. The common verdict is that nowhere else can so much be found which appeals to the seeker for health and quiet 'near to nature's heart.'

Children's amusements. [· · · '· · ·· ·- ·t claims of the ch · · · 1·' · · ·· iic· l·:· ·:t· ponies,

saddles and carts for riding and driving; a short golf course
where they will not be a nuisance to expert adult players; extra
wide and safe boats and canoes, scow and raft, and a special
swimming beach with shallow water where smooth hard sand
slopes so gradually that they can wade out many rods without
danger; there is also a great stone dock, 50x150 ft, sand coverd,
with 13 ft board walk round it   Here they may bathe, dive,
wade, fish, sail boats, play in the clean sand and make all the
noise they wish.   They have also their own croquet and tennis
courts; regular music for children's dancing at different hours;
children's pavilion or 'squealery' with no restrictions on noise
or frolic, as there are no rooms above or below.   This can be
inclosed in glass on 3 sides and has radiators for chilly weather
In 1901 there was added a playhouse on the children's beach,
large enough to shelter the whole troop from sun or rain.
There are swings of various patterns, seesaws, children's oar-
penter shop, scores of indoor and outdoor games, sand heaps,
fresh hay and many things delightful to healthy boys and girls,
so that the club is justly known as the 'children's paradise'
because their needs are constantly borne in mind.   The best
juvenil books and periodicals are in the club library   Traind
kindergartners at moderate cost take entire charge of children
a part of each day   Bird classes and other forms of nature
study under skild guidance in the fields and woods are similarly
offerd.   All this attracts the children and is a great relief to
mothers.

Outdoors.   Most resorts have a single mountain, outlook,
lake, river, beach or bit of forest, a single walk or drive or
picnic ground   Lake Placid has an embarrassment of riches in
its manifold outdoor attractions.   It is common remark from
old travelers that no other point combines so many and that 20
ordinary resorts could be completely equipt from the abundance
which nature has lavisht on this choice spot.   An unbroken
coronet of peaks surrounds the entire valley, which is fild with
nature's attractions in almost endless variety.

Maps.   The small maps issued by the club and the rail-
roads are free.   The old standard map of the Adirondacks,
revised annually for 30 years, is S. R. Stoddard's; on linen
paper, folded and bound for the pocket. $1.   The U. S. Geo-
logic survey issues at cost, 5c each, 47x55 cm sheets of its great

topografic map with very full details for each locality. The new state map of Lake Placid and vicinity by Verplanck Colvin, which is now printing, is more accurate and has fuller and later data. All desirable maps of the region are for sale at both Clubhouse and Lodge.

Lodge. Adirondack Lodge with its 50 miles of trails thru the forest to the finest scenery of eastern America has been known for 20 years as the best point of the Adirondacks for camping parties and mountain climbing. This will be made one of the club's great specialties hereafter. Mr Henry van Hoevenberg, who built the Lodge, has been made club forester and will be in residence to afford any needed assistance to club members young or old. A carriage will run regularly each way between club and Lodge, materially reducing labor and expense of making these most famous excursions, and opening the way for more outdoor life in the 'Heart of the Adirondacks.' At the Lodge there will be Wednesday night camp-fire stories and refreshments and at the club the cathedral and lake fires.

The Lodge, with famous Mt Jo, Clear or Heart lake and the surrounding forest, was bo't in October 1900 and has been restord, renovated and refitted as the forest branch of the club. It is 10 miles from Clubhouse on the site selected from the entire forest as best deserving the name which all visitors gladly accord to it, 'Heart of the Adirondacks.' Yet in this

Lake Placid Club   Adirondack Lodge   Heart of the Adirondacks   105

retreat may now be had complete home comforts combined
with forest wildness. Hot and cold water, baths, lavatories,
and closets have been added to each floor and the table and
beds are the best. The special Lodge circular ' L ' gives details
of the scores of excursions to be made satisfactorily only from
this starting point.   Baedeker, the most famous guidebook,
pronounces some of this scenery about the Lodge and the
Indian and Avalanche passes among the grandest in the New
World. Others say it is second only to Niagara.

Moose island. The central and largest island in Lake
Placid. It rises from the water on a regular slope to the center
390 feet above the lake. It is all virgin forest and includes

Club's Moose island from Eagle's Eyrie

some of the most beautiful woods in the Adirondacks, with
many great rocks, mossy ravines and other picturesque features. On these 500 acres there are miles of beautiful beaches
and wooded shore front where the water is deep enough to allow
steamboats or launches to land. It is in the very center of the
mountains, looking out on Whiteface, St Armand, Eagle's
Eyrie, McKenzie, Overlook, Pulpit and the cluster of peaks at
the north end of the lake. Of this view Wallace's guide says:
'The northern end of Lake Placid is specially bold and impos-
ing. The primeval forest stretches from the rocky shore to the
surrounding mountain tops, and water, islands, wood and ever
changing sky conspire to charm the senses.'

Landings at convenient points open the way to the summit and other attractiv points. Steamers stop on signal without extra charge at any dock on any trip, and numerous landings for small boats make the whole island conveniently accessible.

Undercliff with its score of cottages is only a pistol shot across the water. While not open to the general public, by courtesy of the management, members of the club may, till it has its own buildings on Moose island, get meals, boats and other accommodations at Undercliff when needed.

Between Overlook and Moose island, Lake Placid

Overlook. 200 acres including the small mountain adjoining Whiteface inn, reacht by boat either thru Sunset or Shelter straits or just at the end of the trail thru the pines, the only path along the shores of Placid, and of the Whiteface inn road, the only carriageway into the forest in this direction. Wallace's guide says 'From the summit only a half mile from the house, and easily attain, may be witnest one of the grandest panoramas the region offers, embracing the whole scenery of the principal giants of the Adirondack range.' From this point the islands seem to cut Placid into 5 lakes. On these 200 acres are 3 picturesque trout brooks, the largest being the best available supply for the village of mountain spring water. A summer house or camp will later be built on Overlook for shelter in sudden storms and as a place to lunch or rest or read.

West hights. 250 acres on west side of Mirror lake, beginning on the summit of Grand View hill and including the entire slope to the west and south, meadows, young pines and balsams, and the woods thru which flow East and West Placid outlets, and highlands beyond. Bo't for the club home before it was thought possible to secure Morningside and now held for another club or private cottages under park restrictions. To this wild park will be added roads, walks, seats and carriage and foot bridges. It offers a fine field for those who enjoy making wild wood paths better than shooting deer or catching trout.

Protection of grounds and woods. Use of club property is limited to members and those holding privilege cards. Our grounds are a private park and no member will disfigure them any more than he would the lawn of his own home. Members who have friends in or near Placid who would enjoy the freedom of the grounds, can get privilege cards from the trustees. Picnickers must not mark their lunching places with scatterd papers, egg shells or other scraps. Such debris may easily and without tools be buried under rocks or roots of trees, or carried back in the lunch baskets. Fires to burn it must not be lighted in the woods.

Outdoor fires. Lighting fires except on the stone piers provided or with special permission from the trustees, is absolutely prohibited on any part of the club grounds or forest. Serious damage has been done by well-meaning people who do not understand the great precautions necessary to keep fire from running underground in the Adirondacks. Members will not only observe the rule themselves but warn others who might violate it. The state law is severe in its penalties for such carelessness, and there are local state fire wardens to enforce it. In many sections a forest fire once started might destroy every building with attendant danger to life. The club buildings are so situated that they are in no danger from this source, but its woods will be protected to the full extent of the law against fires, cutting or mutilating trees or shrubs, specially white birches, or other acts of trespass.

Departments. Boating and Golf as great specialties were made distinct departments. In 1901 Driving is put on the same plane, and under the head Nature a distinct department is devoted to mountain climbing, camping and field work, and exploration in study of this wonderful region. Other outdoor recreations, games and sports and general athletics are groupt in department A.

Walks. Walking parties make all the trips under 'Drives' and 'Mountains' and have left almost unlimited possibilities. Over 50 miles of trails have already been opend, and are put in repair each season. These trails are extended every year in order to enable those who do not care for a wild scramble thru unbroken forest to reach the most attractiv points. They are narrow forest trails to be followd comfortably only in indian file A partial list of short walks is given as suggestiv. Most parties allow an hour for each 3 miles tho very rapid walkers can travel faster without over-exertion. Arrangement is in order of distance except that circles are given first. Those wishing clearer directions as to roads, trails and other features can obtain any one of the 5 different maps of the club region at Clubhouse or Lodge.

The map of the grounds about the central clubhouse shows scores of short walks in Morningside. The public club buildings are common points for walks, but if a whole cottage is taken it becomes private and club members call only on friends exactly as if the cottage were not ownd by the club.

The circles Starting back from lake near Northwood on Hillcrest road, walks of varying lengths are made by following the successiv roads to the right leading back to the lake. There is a score of variations on these most common loops.

'*Round the Pines.*' By Pines road, Plateau, Cabin, Pines grove and Hillcrest road. ½ m.

Hillcrest circle. Brookwood road over Uplands between Balsams and Pines, over Hillcrest and to Mirror lake between Edgewater and Orchard. 1 m.

Bonniebrae. Edgewood road, 2½ m, round the golf links, Wilmington road, 3½ m.

Round Mirror lake. By Lakeshore drive 3 m. This winds round Mirror lake. The beach or Edgewater trail is also being built at the very edge of the water, screend from the road by trees and shrubbery.

Forestview circle Placid hights, Valleyview, Overbrook and round club golf links by highway. 4 m.

Restend lake-grove. Hammocks and seats at the quiet end between highway and lake. 1-6 m.

Hillcrest tower. On summit east of Clubhouse. Wonderful view varying with hour and cloud effects. ¼ m.

Ondawa rock. Beyond Pines cabin, across the tiny Ondawa valley to rock and natural birch arbor. ¼ m.

Brookwood spring. In edge of Brookwood near Forest courts. Discoverd by a surveyor who reported it the finest spring water he had found in 20 years in the forest. Made accessible and used exclusivly on club tables tho all the hotels and houses of the village are supplied from the lake, where both water companies get all their water. ¼ m.

Whiteface slope. By Brookwood road or from Uplands down hill over Meadowbrook bridge. This side of Brookwood, dotted with young pines and balsams, slopes to the north with fine view of Whiteface. ⅜ m.

Big balsam. Largest balsam tree which the state botanist and the sup't of forests have found. 5 minutes south from Brookwood spring, near Edgewood road. ⅜ m.

Greenacre grove. Favorit out-of-door seats on north edge of golf links just beyond Forest courts and Valley Forge. ⅜ m.

Mirror lake overlook. Highest point in Lakewood, near golf landing. ⅜ m.

Lakewood. By boat to golf landing or lake shore drive or thru Wayside wood by Forest, Woodbine and Clematis or thru Valley Forge or station roads. South end of Clubhouse grounds, most convenient stroll in the shady woods. ⅜ m.

Rushmora. Under big pines at south end of lake across outlet on rustic bridge. ½ m; by boat, ⅜ m.

Camp Sentinel photografic studio. East of Pines grove. ½ m.

Bonniebrae. Charming nooks for naps or books under trees on wooded slope at south end of Brookwood vista, between Valleyview and Meadowbrook, reacht from Whiteface slope, or by Edgewood road from Forest courts or by Brookwood spring trail to Big balsam. ½ m.

Theanoguen, Eastgate and Colden. Via Brookwood vista, Edgewood road or golf links, Placid hights manor house. ½ m.

Golf houses. By golf path, thru Forest courts, Midwood, and Green... Favorit resort in the late afternoon when shadows are playing on Sentinel range. Finest sunset views in the mountains. ½ m.

Titans. 2 largest pines of section in Southwood, a few steps south from Valley road from lake to golf house. ½ m.

Camp Herbert. . This photografic studio has produced the finest Adirondack views yet taken. On north shore of Mirror lake By boat or lake shore drive, ⅔ m.

Water hazards and trout ponds. On Meadowbrook, near Wilmington road ¾ m.

Overbrook Evergreen grove southeast from golf houses ¾ m.

Hotel Ruisseaumont. On shore of Placid, surrounded by picturesque cottages. 1 m.

Little Cobble or Altar mountain. ½ m east of Clubhouse, pretty forest trail with short, sharp climb at end; a famous view easily reacht. Specially fine near sunset. 2 hours should be allowd for leisurely trip 1 m.

Old Forge ravine. Elba river, south of golf links. 1 m.

Railroad station. 1 m.

Ruisseaumont steamer landing. 1¼ m

Pulpit mountain or Mt Whitney. The low mountain northeast from Ruisseaumont; path leads from hotel to outlook tower on summit, commanding a fine view. 1¼ m.

Old Forge plateau. Precipitious south bank of Elba river. These pastures out in the open, command fine mountain views in all directions. Entrance from Keene road at Old Forge lodge. 1½ m.

Western pines. Slope from West hights near Grand View hotel to Outlet valley, dotted with beautiful young pines. Thru it are trails to Lake Placid and North Elba water works. 1½ m; by boat ¾ m.

Village. Steamboat landing or Lake Placid carry, churches, hotels, cottages, stores, and postoffice, on west side of Mirror lake, 1 to 1½ m; by boat less than ½ m.

Village public library. 1½ m; by boat ⅓ m.

Club steam laundry. 1½ m; by boat ⅜ m.

Westside lakehouse and club bowling alleys. 1½ m; by boat ⅓ m.

St Eustace church   Near steamboat landing and carry on north slope of Signal hill, near best viewpoint between lakes. 1½ m; by boat to St Eustace landing ½ m.

Ridge road.   Thru forest from Grand View to Stevens house.   1¾ m; by boat 1 m

Club farms.   Edgehill, 2 m; Highland 2½ m; Elba Inn 2 m.

Outlet valley, rivers and water works.   Below western pines.   2 m.

Cornhill.   Easy climb to fine local view on Club's Elba Inn farm   2¼ m

Highfield.   Crossing rustic bridges near water works, thru forest to fine views from clearing at west, back by Westwood way   2½ m; by boat 1¾ m.

Whiteface golf links.   On new Saranac road.   2½ m; by boat 2 m.

Iron bridge and lower steam sawmill.   On Lodge road. Pretty valley beyond Keene road racecourse, on edge of John Brown's farm.   3 m.

John Brown's grave.   3 m

Ling steam sawmill.   Beyond club farms.   3 m.

Maple hill.   Fine maple grove on old Saranac road or may be reacht by new Westwood way across outlets and thru pastures.   3 m.

Moose island.   By boat to Crescent bay, Picnic rock, Hopping bear point or east shore, thru primeval forests with beautiful trees, great rocks and mossy ravines   The island is only 5 miles in circumference so there is no danger as in mainland forest of getting lost, as one is sure to find the lake shore in some direction   A favorit place for a quiet day and for camping.   3 m

Overlook.   Club's mountain of 200 acres west of Whiteface inn, 3 beautiful brooks, a hardwood forest and near the summit a view famous in the guide books as one of the best in the Adirondacks.   The islands seem to make 5 small lakes at one's feet.   A plain trail breaks into the forest from the highway opposit the inn stables.   To the inn by steamer or rowboat, carriage road, bicycle path or the 'trail thru the pines' along the lake shore.   A full half day's trip.   Many prefer to carry lunches and take more time.   By road 4 miles; by boat 2½ m.

Eagle's eyrie. By boat to Echo bay, an hour's climb up a beautiful brook to a marvelous panorama of the lakes and mountains to the south, printed on p. 28 of Handbook. 6 m.

There are walks in every direction leading to beautiful views or charming retreats in the forest so that one may walk all summer and still have new places to explore within easy distance of Clubhouse.

Mountain climbing. This region is unsurpast in attractions for this most fascinating, exhilarating and healthful outdoor exercise. There are scores of mountains, low and high, with excellent, well-markt trails, and hundreds of others for those who prefer to test their woodcraft and endurance by finding their way thru pathless forests. The views obtaind are justly famous and well repay the effort. By common consent the finest views in the state are to be had from the high peaks nearest Lake Placid. From Whiteface no less than 65 lakes have been counted including Champlain and Ontario. Experienced and trusty guides can always be had but parties are made up every day of the season of those who prefer to take the safer and easier trips alone. Substantial lunches are provided with needed conveniences from a mere basket and drinking cup to a complete camping outfit. The chief advice is to go slow. Young climbers usually tire themselves out the first of the trip till they learn the practical wisdom of the guides, who never hurry up hill. Frequent rests at good points for views or in

shady nooks take a little time but make the day easy, specially
for ladies and those unaccustomd to vigorous exercise. The
tonic of the air is so great that many who think it quite impossible to climb find they have the necessary strength. Trips of
3 or 4 hours are usually made before or after dinner. For
longer ones it is better to take lunch to eat on the summit
where the party rests during the middle of the day. The
check list of 90 peaks below only partly represents the wealth
of the region. There are over 200 mountains within 15 miles
air line from Clubhouse, any one of which would be named and
visited often at other resorts where it was not lost in the multi-
tude of peaks. Similarly the 147 lakes and other features in
the 2d list omit an even larger number of which we do not
know the names.

Peak of Whiteface

Guides. The most important element in the success of
many trips is a competent, sober, trustworthy and personally
agreeable guide. Both at Clubhouse and Adirondack Lodge
such guides are regularly employd. If extra ones are needed
they can be found easiest and best by applying at the office.

CHECK LIST OF NATURAL FEATURES WITHIN 15 MILE RADIUS OF
CLUBHOUSE

Mountains

	HIGHT	MILES DISTANT	DIRECTION
Adams	3500	14	S
Algonquin (McIntire)	5112	10	S
Allen	4345	15	S
Ampersand	3432	11	WSW
Armstrong	4455	13	SSE
Bald	2120	16	SE
Bartlett ridge	3880	15	SSE
Basin	4825	12	SSE
Bassett	1954	11½	ENE
Baxter	2400	11	ESE
Bear den	3423	14	SE
Big crow	2820	12	ESE
Big slide	4255	9	SSE
Cascade	4092	7	SE
Catamount	3168	13	NNE
Clark	1577	15	NE
Clematis	2540	12	E
Cliff	4000	14	S
Clinton	4938	11	S
Cobble	2330	1	NE
Colden	4713	11	S
Colvin	4074	15	SSE
Dial	4023	15	SE
Dix	4842	16	SSE
Eagle's Eyrie	2656	4¾	NNE
Ebenezer	1960	11	ENE
Esther	4270	8	NE
Fremont hill	1859	16	NNE
Giant	4622	16	SE
Gothic	4738	12½	SSE
Green		15	ESE
Hamlin	2122	14	NE
Haystack	4918	13	ENE
Hedgehog	?4000	11	SE
Henderson	3000	14	SSW

	HIGHT	MILES DISTANT	DIRECTION
Hopkins	3136	13	ESE
Hurricane	3687	14	ESE
Indian face	2500	14	SSE
Iroquois (McIntire range)		11	S
Jay		16	ENE
Jo	2870	10	S
Knap hill	2328	8½	N
Knoblock	3184	15½ ·	ESE
Legett		11	NNE
Lime kiln	2925	16	ESE
Little crow	2697	12	ESE
Long pond	2268	8	ESE
McDonough	3800	15	E
McIntire (Algonquin)	-5112	10	S
McKenzie	3189	5	NW
Marble	2725	9	NE
Marcy (Tahawus)	5344	12	SSE
Moose pond		7	NNW
Morgan		12	NE
Nippletop	4620	15½	SSE
Noonmark	3552	14½	SE
Nye		6	
Oak ridge	2490	11	ESE
Overlook		2½	NNW
Owl's head	2165	8	ESE
Panther	2600	15	SSW
Pitchoff	2750	15	ESE
Porter	'4070	6½	SE
Pulpit (Whitney)	2658	1½	NNE
Rattlesnake knob	1968	11	ENE
Redfield	4606	14	S
Red rock	2490	11	ESE
Rooster comb	2795	11	SE
Round	3145	15	SE
Saddleback	4530	12	SSE
Saddleback (Jay)	3623	15	E
Santanoni	4644	16	SSW
Sawteeth (Resagonia)	4138	14	SSE
Sentinel peak	3858	6½	ENE

	HIGHT	MILES DISTANT	DIRECTION
Seward	4384	14	SW
Skylight	4920	13½	S
Spread eagle	2860	11	SE
Street	3300	7	
Summit rock		11	SSW
Tabletop	4440	10	SSE
Tahawus (Marcy)	5344	12	SE
Tripod	3340	15	ESE
Twin mountains	?3500	9	SE
Wainwright	1633	12½	ENE
Wallface	3893	11	SSW
Whiteface	4872	6½	NNE
Whitney (Pulpit)	2658	1½	NNE
Wolf's jaws	4175	12	SE
Wright	4000	9	S

Lakes, ponds, passes, falls, etc.

	MILES DISTANT	DIRECTION
Alder brook	15	N
Ampersand brook	12½	WSW
" pond	11	WSW
Arnold, Lake	11½	SSE
Ausable lake, lower	16	SE
" upper	16	SSE
Ausable river, east branch	9½	E
" west branch	2	E
Avalanche lake	11	S
" pass	(?) 11	S
Bartlett's carry	16	W
Big cherrypatch pond	2	E
Black pond	14½	W
Bouquet river	16	SE
Brown's brook	13	NE
Buck island	1½	N
Bushnell falls	11	SSE
Calamity pond	13	S
Camus pond	6	WSW
Cascade lakes	:	SE
Chapel pond	10	SE

	MILES DISTANT	DIRECTION
Clear (Heart) lake	7	S
Clear pond	13½	WNW
Clifford brook .	6	E
Clifford falls	8	ESE
Colby pond	9	WNW
Cold brook .	7	WSW
"	12	S
Colden, Lake	12	S
Coldspring pond	3½	NE
Cole brook	12	N
Connery pond	2½	NE
Copperas pond	5	NE
Cranberry pond	13	NE
Crystal brook	15	SSE
Dial pond	16	SE
Dipper, Giant's	16	SE
East branch Ausable river	9½	E
Echo lake (Lake of the golden lilies)	¾	NE
Elba river	1	S
Elk pass	15½	SE
Feldspar brook	13	S
Flume	8	NE
Franklin falls	11	N
French's brook	12	NE
Giant's dipper	16	SE
" washbowl	16	SE
Gill brook	14	SE
Gravestone brook .	15½	SE
Gulf brook .	12	ESE
Harkness, Lake	16	SSW
Hawk island	3½	NNE
Haystack brook	15	SSE
Heart (Clear) lake	7	S
Henderson, Lake	13½	SSW
High falls	7	NE
Hunter's pass	16	SE
Indian carry	16	WSW
" pass	1)	SSW·
Isham pond		SE

	MILES DISTANT	DIRECTION
John's brook	11	SE
Jones pond	15	NW
Lake, *see distinctiv name*		
Lake of the golden lilies (Echo)	¾	NE
Little Ampersand pond	9½	W
" black brook	15	NE
" cherrypatch pond	2	ENE
" clear pond	15½	WNW
" Weller pond	14	W
Livingston pond	13	S
Lochbonnie	4	NNW
Lonesome pond	8½	W
Long pond	3	NE
Loon bay	11½	W
Lost pond	14	ESE
Lower Ausable lake	16	SE
" Saranac lake	9	WNW
" twin brook	15	S
McAultey pond	11	WNW
McIntire brook	7½	S
McKenzie pond	6	NW
Malcom pond	3	E
Marcy brook	7½	S
Marsh pond	5	NE
Miller pond	8	W
Moose island	2¼	N
" pond	6½	NW
" "	9½	SW
Morgan pond	12	NE
Moss pond	15	SSE
Mud pond (Echo)	¾	NE
New bridge brook	13	NE
O'Connell brook	12	E
Opalescent river	12	S
Ore bed brook	11	SSE
Otis brook	13	NE
Owen pond	4½	NE
Pine pond	9	W
Pope bay	10¹·	W

	MILES DISTANT	DIRECTION
Preston ponds	13	SW
Rainbow fall .	13½	SSE
" lake	15	NNW
Ray brook	5	W
Robinson pond	5	WSW
Rocky branch	14	ENE
Round lake	5½	SE
"	13	W
Russel fall	13	SE
Saginaw bay	15	W
St Regis lake, upper	15½	NNW
Sally, Lake	15	SSW
Sanford, Lake	15½	SSW
Saranac falls	13	W
Saranac lake, lower	9	WNW
" upper	15½	W
Scott ponds	10	SSW
Shingle boy pond	11	WNW
Silver lake	15	NNE
Skylight brook	15	SSE
Slide brook	10	SE
Slide mountain brook	10	SSE
South meadow brook	6½	SE
Still brook	6	N
Stony creek pond	16	W
Style's brook	11	E
Sunrise notch	6	NE
Surprise, Lake (Echo)	¾	NE
Taylor pond	14	NNE
Tear in the clouds, Lake	13	S
Thompson brook	4	SE
Tom Peck pond	2¼	NE
Twin brook, lower	15	S
" upper	14	S
Uphill brook	13	S
Upper Ausable lake	16	SSE
" St Regis lake	15½	WNW
" Saranac lake	15½	W
" twin "	¼	S

	MILES DISTANT	DIRECTION
Wallface ponds	12	SSW
Warren pond	4½	NE
Washbowl, Giant's	16	SE
Weller pond	14	W
West branch Ausable river	2	E
Wilmington high falls	7	NE
Wilmington notch	5	NE
Woodruff falls	12	NNE
Wynch pond	5½	NE

Cycling. Those used to city parkways and macadamized drives may think the best mountain roads very poor, yet many all-year residents now ride constantly, and visitors bring and enjoy their wheels greatly. Others have never learnd the art or charm of dodging about country lanes for a smooth hard track, and so seldom ride. The favorit short rides are the 3 miles round Mirror lake, 3 miles round the club links and Forestview, 7 miles to Whiteface Inn or 6 to John Brown's grave and back. Wheelmen make all the trips under 'Drives' and also push out on each of the 3 great highways leading out of Placid valley: 1) Wilmington road, northeast toward Lake

Champlain; 2) Keene road by Cascade lakes and Keene to Elizabethtown and Westport-on-Champlain; 3) Saranac road. The maps of the L. A. W. show the cycle roads about Lake Placid to be the best in the mountains. Recent substantial progress has been made and every year increases the amount of good cycling. Local interest is shown by the well advanced 10-mile sidepath between Lake Placid and Saranac, which was the

Club road from station

most sandy road. This is half done and completion is promist in 1901. There is a special cycle room for members' wheels at the club boat livery, the best high or low priced bicycles are for sale or rent and members can have their own wheels stord, cleand or repaird.

Cooperation. The receipts from driving, boating, golf and other recreations for which a charge is made are spent wholly on these departments, on which no one makes a profit.

Driving. Placid is well known as the driving center of the Adirondacks. Members fond of this recreation felt that the club should have its own stables, maintaining the high standards which characterize its boating facilities. Therefore in

1901 driving was made a leading club specialty and the best
stable in the region was built and equipt for taking the best
care of favorit horses.   It has box stalls, wash racks, harness
room, drivers library and reading room, livery room, office,
salesroom, 2 floors of drivers rooms with hot and cold water,
porcelain bath, closets and lavatories.   It also provides for
those who would bring choice horses and carriages if they had
satisfactory accommodations instead of the ordinary hotel
stables, and they can now have light, dry, well ventilated quarters in charge of responsible, experienced men.   15 new Waterloo carriages, with high backs and broad seats, 20 new Troy
harnesses, 20 new horses, and complete new furnishings, as for

Lake Placid Club   Lakewood drive

a first class private stable, have been added to the equipment
of 1900.   There is a new manager and experienced drivers and
stablemen, and constant study is made to secure the highest
safety and comfort and to furnish a higher grade of horses and
more satisfactory turnouts than are elsewhere obtainable.
There will be offerd this year various facilities impracticable
in a public hotel but very desirable for a club because they
give it more the character of a private estate.

As in club boats, unusual provision is made for various
wants and tastes.   Besides the usual livery there are for ladies
and children safe and gentle Shetland and other ponies and
horses for carts, phaetons, buckboards and surries, all chosen

specially for this work. For skilful drivers there are higher-lived horses with suitable handsome turnouts which can be had by the month or day, thus affording facilities which can usually be enjoyd only in a fine private stable. These however will positivly not be let without drivers except to those competent

A Placid drive

and willing to give such horses proper care on trying mountain roads. Any other course would soon ruin the horses so that even careful drivers would have nothing but the overworkt and broken down. These best turnouts are refused for private driving to any one who has taild to bring the horses back in

satisfactory condition.   However skilful and experienced,
drivers who believe in 'putting them thru and buying more
when these are worn out' and the larger class who believe
themselves competent but really know little about horses, must

High falls, Wilmington road

not expect to use without
drivers those provided
only for amateur horsemen who are both careful
and competent.   A spe-
cial feature is pair driving
on light wagon roads or
buckboards.   To encour-
age this the charge for a
pair will be not double
but only one half more
than for single.   This
year 3 new 2-seat surries
have been added for ladies
to drive with children or
light loads on the level
roads about the lake.
These are not let for long
drives or hard roads, but only for easy driving by careful people
who prefer to have their own turnouts without a driver and
wish to make up little family parties.   These are specially de-
signd for those who wish to make weekly or monthly rates for
the whole or partial use of such family carriages

Saddle horses.   Most stables are forced to give up keeping saddle horses entirely because so many are ruind by over-
riding.   Hard and fast riders who wish to gallop up and down
hill must bring their own horses or get them elsewhere.   For
those willing to give good horses careful usage, the club provides for men, women and children.   For others it will order
promptly from the livery stables the best to be had but will not
allow its own horses to be spoild for those for whom they were
bo't even if the rule offends some very delightful people who
are 'hard on horses.'

Driving equipment.   For economy and to secure exactly
what is wisht some prefer to own their horses or to hire by the
month and treat as private turnouts.   After careful inquiry we

selected the Waterloo Wagon Co and the Troy Harness Co. as the best makers, considering high quality and product and reasonable prices   A salesroom in the stable provides a liberal assortment of carriages, harnesses and all needed articles for immediate delivery and at the least obtainable prices.   Horses are also for sale or for rent by the week, month or season, with or without drivers.   Families will find this the most economical and satisfactory method specially if 2 or more members divide the cost of a horse or pair.

Driving price list.   A convenient list on which members can check off drives taken in exploration of the surrounding country.   The prices given cover only cooperativ cost of maintaining the club stables at the new high standard   The horses earn these prices only a few weeks but must be fed for 52. Hay and oats are very high in the mountains because of high freights.   Nearly all hotels find it unprofitable to carry on stables at these rates, and farm out the business to liverymen. The club tried this plan 5 years but could not get as good equipment or service as its members properly demand in surroundings so picturesquely adapted to much driving.

Printed prices are invariable for grade A or best horses, drivers and Waterloo, Glens Falls, buckboards, the most luxurious and easy riding of these famous carriages, but for mountain wagons and other grade B or older or cheaper turnouts lower rates may be made for drive, week or month   A lower rate may be given for long trips if teams can be spared and are to return without passengers.   For 2 horses on 1-seat carriage deduct ¼ from price of 3-seat.

		Round trip miles	GLENS FALLS		
			1-seat	2-seat	3-seat
Any trip under 5 miles			$1	$1 75	$2
Adirondack lodge	half day	20	3	5	6
	whole "		4	7	8
Adirondack sanitarium	half day	24	3 50	6	7
	whole "		4	7	8
" summer art school		16	3	5	6
Ames's (Mountain View)		12	2	3.50	4
Ampersand hotel	half day	24	3 50	6	7
	whole "		4	"	8

		Round trip miles	GLENS FALLS		
			1-seat	2-seat	3-seat
Ausable chasm	2 days	78	10	$17.50	$20
	3 "		12	21	24
Ausable Forks, pulp mills	2 "	50	8	14	16
" via Keene	2 "	62	8	14	16
Ausable lakes	2 "	56	8	14	16
Averyville		12	2	3 50	4
Beede's (St Hubert's)	2 days	48	8	14	16
Black Brook	2 "	48	8	14	16
Bloomingdale	1 day	37	6	10.50	12
	2 days		8	14	16
Bluff pt, Hotel Champlain	2 "	51	8	14	16
Cascade lakes	half day	20	3	5	6
	whole "		4	7	8
East hill (Prof Davidson's)	1 day	39	6	10 50	12
	2 days		8	14	16
Edgehill farm		3	1	1 75	2
Edgehill triangle		5	1	1 75	2
Elizabetht'n, via Keene	2 days	56	8	14	16
" Upper Jay	2 "	60	8	14	16
Euba mills	2 "	60	8	14	16
" via Elizabetht'n	2 "	76	10	17 50	20
	3 "		12	21	24
Forest View circle		4	1	1.75	2
Franklin Falls	2 days	48	8	14	16
Freeman's home		16	3	5	6
Glenmore, East hill	1 day	39	6	10 50	12
Grand View		3	1	1 75	2
Highland farm		5	1	1.75	2
Hotel Champlain	2 days	51	8	14	16
Iron bridge on W Ausable		6	1 25	2	2 50
Jay, via Keene	2 "	52	8	14	16
" Wilmington	1 day	38	6	10 50	12
	2 days		8	14	16
John Brown's grave		8	1.50	2 50	3
Keene Center		32	4	7	8
Keene hights	2 "	50	8	14	16
Keene Valley	1 day	42	6	10 50	12
	2 days		8	14	16

	Round trip	miles	GLENS FALLS 1-seat	2-seat	3-seat
Keeseville	2 days	72	$10	$17.50	$20
	3 "		12	21	24
Lake Clear (Rice's)		25	4	7	8
Lake Placid house		3	1	1.75	2
Loon Lake (Chase's)	2 days	56	8	14	16
Lower Jay		30	4	7	8
McKenzie pond		16	3	5	6
Mineville	2 days	76	10	17.50	20
	3 "		12	21	24
Miss Newman's farm	.	12	2	3.50	4
Miss Newman's roadend		14	2 50	4	5
Mountain View (Ames's)		12	2	3.50	4
Newman		2	1	1 75	2
New Russia	2 days	64	9	16	18
North Elba p. o.		8	1 50	2 50	3
Paul Smith's	2 days	52	8	14	16
Port Henry	3 "	90	12	21	24
Port Kent	3 "	84	12	21	24
Rainbow lake (Wardner's)	1 day	28	4	7	8
Ray Brook house (Cameron's)		12	2	3.50	4
Riverside drive (Ausable circle)		10	2	3.50	4
Round Mirror lake		3	1	1 75	2
Round Saranac square		10	2	3 50	4
Ruisseaumont		2	1	1 75	2
St Eustace P E church		3	1	1 75	2
St Gabriel's sanit'm (R C)	2 days	56	8	14	16
St Hubert's inn	2 "	48	8	14	16
Saranac Inn	2 days	52	8	14	16
Saranac Lake (vill. or r r.)	half day	20	3	5	6
	whole "		4	7	8
Ampersand, Algonquin or sanitarium	half day	24	3 50	6	7
	whole "		4	7	8
Signal hill		3	1	1 75	2
Silver lake	2 days	66	9	16	18
South Meadows	half day	20	3	5	6
	whole "		4	7	8
Steamboat landing		3	1	1 75	2
Stevens house		3	1	1 75	2

		Round trip miles	GLENS FALLS		
			1-seat	2-seat	3-seat
Summer school of art		16	$3	$5	$6
Summer school of philosophy	1 day	39	6	10 50	12
Union Falls,	2 days	60	8	14	16
Upper Jay, via Keene	2 "	44	8	14	16
" Wilm'gt'n	2 "	46	8	14	16
Westport	2 "	72	10	17 50	20
	3 "		12	21	24
White church square		5	1	1 75	2
Whiteface golf links		5	1	1 75	2
Whiteface inn ·		8	1.50	2 50	3
Willey house (East hill)	1 day	38	6	10.50	12
	2 days		8	14	16
Wilmington flume		25	4	7	8
Wilmington high falls	half day	20	3	5	6
	whole "		4	7	8
Wilmington-Keene sq.	2 days	45	8	14	16
Wilmington village		30	4	7	8
Wood farm (Adirondack lodge road)		12	2	3.50	4

Prices are at the rate of 20c a mile for saddle horse or single, 35c for double, 40c for 3-seat carriages and 12½c for Shetland or other ponies with cart or saddle. '

Prices to places not on the list are fixt by this table:

		Pony cart	1-seat or saddle horse	2-seat	3-seat
Under	5 miles	$ .75	$1	$1 75	$2
	7	1	1 25	2	2.50
	8	1	1.50	2 50	3.
	9	1.25	1 75	3	3 50
	12	1.50	2	3 50	4
	14	1.75	2 50	4	5
	16	2	3	5	6
	18	2 25	3.50	6	7
	30 in 1 day	2 50	4	7	8

4-horse drag, break or hayride rack double 3-seat price.

Experienced drivers attend all double teams. Single carriages with 1 or 2 horses will be let without drivers only to competent and careful horsemen. They may also arrange to drive their own 2-seat teams by special permit if they observe the club rules for driving and bring the horses back in good condition.

Meals for drivers and horses when away from home are paid for by the club and drivers have positiv orders not to postpone unduly the feeding of its horses. Club and Lodge horses are cared for free at either stables Visitors to the Lodge save expense by going in by club teams

Only 5 miles an hour is practicable on these mountain roads without injury to most horses. 20 miles, or one third more than the stage line average, is allowd for a full day's work. Horses are expected to do only 100 miles a week and overwork of some days is balanced by corresponding rest. Except in emergencies no club team is driven more than 30 miles (or double stage line work) in any 1 day. A 'half day' is before 1 p. m , between 1 and 6 p. m. or after 5 p. m. No extra charge is made for overtime not exceeding 1 hour

All prices are by miles traveld, not by time. If distance traveld averages less than 2½ miles an hour because of stops the charge is by the hour at half usual rate or 50c single, $1 double; e. g. a horse kept 8 hours would be charged for 20 miles or a full day tho he was driven a less distance.

All prices are by nearest roads to points named If extra distance is traveld it is enterd on slip on return and charged at printed schedule rates. No charge is made till this report of trip is made after return.

Prices by week or month. Horses and carriages for exclusiv use, with driver, club assuming all risks.

	Week	Month
pony and cart	$12.50	$50
saddle	20	80
1-seat carriage, 1 horse	20	80
" " 2 horses	30	120
2-seat " "	35	140
3-seat " "	40	160

Board. Board for private horses $1 a day; in box stalls $1.50 a day. Those furnishing their own grooms are allowd 25c a day for each horse.

Transfers. To railway station, steamboat landing, opera house, Club golf links or any Mirror lake hotel or church, in mountain wagons 25c, in Glens Falls carriages 50c each person,

each way, unless return is made immediately without stop, when
no return fare is charged.   These prices do not apply for less
than 2 fares for buggy, 3 fares for 2-seat, 5 fares for 3-seat, i. e.
4 persons would pay $1.25 for a 3-seat carriage

If private carriages are orderd they must be at minimum
rate charged for all drives under 5 miles, $1, $1 75 and $2.

To all trains and all regular Sunday services round trip for
1 or more persons 25c each in transfers, 50c in carriages.

Transfer of trunks 25c each.   Club checks will be given
for both inward and outward baggage at the house and station.

Athletic club.   Those interested pay $1 a year and con-
stitute the Morningside athletic club.   All fees and any returns
for use of its outfits or from tournaments or other sources are
used in improving athletic facilities.   This club supplies for a
small fee golf sticks, tennis rackets, roque or croquet mallets
and balls, and other needed articles, and aims to introduce and
foster any outdoor recreations which seem desirable and practicable.   The grounds, woods and lakes afford the best possible
opportunity for all forms of outdoor sports.   The club has the
best location at Placid for both land and water tournaments
and matches, sailing, rowing, paddling and swimming races,
float nights, etc.   The advantages of its great piazzas and
sloping shores with shelterd seats are recognized by all

Subclubs.   These are the simplest possible   Whenever
several members are interested in one thing they naturally
cooperate for promoting that interest and their own convenience
and pleasure in following it.   Membership at present means
little more than that one shares in the recreation, contributes
the trifling fee for incidental expenses and cooperates with others
in advancing the interests of their common pastime.   Rooms
are provided for the occasional meetings needed to plan trips,
matches, tournaments, etc   The Club provides unusual facilities for all these recreations and bears various general expenses.
Each club raises by its annual fees, subscriptions, entertainments or otherwise the small amounts needed for its own incidental expenses.   Some of these clubs will doubtless become
more permanent and activ.   Some will do nothing one year
and much the next, as each usually depends on the activity of
some enthusiastic leader.   If a half dozen persons are specially
fond of boating, tennis, roque, basket ball or any other game,

they agree on certain days and hours and invite others who are players, and the group is known as 'the _____ club,' and all matters pertaining to its special game are referd to it by the trustees. Those who bring their own horses, or hire by the month or day the special club turnouts for fine private driving, are interested in roads, driving parties, stopping places, etc and make a Driving club. The devotees of horseback exercise are the Stirrup club. The Cycle and Walking clubs appeal to those who prefer the wheel or long tramps to horses, and are glad to know others of similar taste likely to join them The Canoe club brings together those fond of paddling, rowing or sailing, the Music and Dramatic clubs those who take pleasure in contributing to the summer's entertainment by utilizing the amateur talent always present but often undiscoverd except by such a club. The Camera club finds scores of enthusiastic photografers glad to know each other's work in a section so rich in material. 3 dark rooms are provided for its use. The Mountain club has as its object exploration and naming of new peaks, cutting needed trails, putting up guideboards and developing in various ways this fascinating and exhilarating outdoor interest From those who engage in each of these recreations the more enthusiastic make the little club which plans various outings in which others not enough interested to join the club and make the plans, are yet glad to share

Track and team athletics. The club field days have been most enjoyable and numerous members of college teams are always present. According to material available and leaders willing to organize, we have a great variety of sports, e. g. long, broad and high jumping, pole vaulting, 3-legged, wheelbarrow, sack, potato, egg and spoon, swimming, obstacle and other races, shot putting, hammer throwing, tug-of-war in boats and on land, walking, swimming, diving, etc.

Suitable programs are provided for children, youths and untraind adults as well as for college athletes, the club physician exercising constant supervision so that there shall be no overstrain. It is the club's settled policy to encourage liberally all wholesome outdoor sports which attract both participants and spectators

Forest courts. These have been graded between Forest and Broo'wood, 5 minutes from Clubhouse on the path to the golf houses. In order to center in one place the various games there is space for 8 full sized courts in ideal surroundings These will be fitted up as fast as needed. On 2 sides are woods which afford shade at all hours to spectators, and which protect from prevailing winds in cold November days and yet leave free circulation of air in warm weather.

Tennis. There is no annoying waiting for courts, as the club has space for 14 games at once.

Tether tennis. Both Forest courts and Lodge have this popular new game.

Roque and croquet. Besides the children's croquet court near the Squealery, courts with rubber cushions for expert play will provide in 1901 for roque, considerd by many the best of all outdoor games, but for which satisfactory facilities for fine play are seldom found. Roque is easily the best outdoor game for those who find golf and tennis too vigorous exercise and the new courts will make it a popular club feature.

Other outdoor sports. The club has already provided facilities for many sports and games and will, whenever a reasonable number wish to take up any desirable new sport, encourage it practically, e g. quoits, archery, handball, lacrosse, cricket, lawn bowls, etc Those interested in starting anything new should consult the treasurer at the club office.

Athletic supplies. The club has the agency for the section of the largest and best makers including A G. Spalding & Bros., Columbia and Spalding bicycles and St Lawrence boats and canoes, and keeps on hand a large assortment for immediate delivery at no advance on city prices. Members save trouble and expense by getting all supplies here instead of bringing from the city. As entire net proceeds of all this business are spent for club outdoor sports it helps our athletic interests to patronize this agency which carries a larger stock than is to be found elsewhere outside large city stores. This includes everything likely to be needed for golf, boating, driving, camping, swimming, cycling, tennis, roque, croquet and other outdoor and indoor sports.

In bicycles there are the 2 best makes, Columbia and Spalding, for men and women, chainless or chain, with either hub or tire coaster brakes. There are also the best lower priced machines and scores of fittings and supplies likely to be needed by some one during the summer. Those not wishing to buy can rent most articles, all receipts going to the athletic club for maintenance of its work.

Rent of clubs, balls, etc. As free provision of rackets, balls, mallets, golf clubs and other appliances led to loss and injury a small fee is charged for the loan of anything needed and a good assortment is kept on hand for sale or rent, the receipts being spent in improving this equipment.

Athletic field. The club has one of the few places in this region where there is enough level space for a satisfactory athletic field. This is half a mile from Clubhouse, conceald by woods, out of sight and sound for those who prefer quiet, but at the end of a pretty wood path for the many who enjoy outdoor sports. A diamond is laid out for baseball and ground assignd for cricket, lawn bowls, and other sports needing ample level space.

Club's ball grounds

Athletic instruction. Vacation days are the best in the year for acquiring any outdoor accomplishment. Competent instructors are seldom available in the country, but the club aims to have them for golf, driving, riding, bicycling, sailing, rowing, canoeing, swimming, etc. In rowing, pupils are taught if wisht with fixt or feathering oars, straight or spoon, with outriggers, sliding seats, single and double sculls and single and double paddles

Swimming school. The club is fortunate in having secured for the entire season the most famous teachers of scientific swimming in this country, Prof. and Mrs Ernest Allen. Needed facilities have been added, swimming trolley, diving pedestal, 32 bath cabins, 400 ft of board walk, so that with best teachers, best water and best conveniences the club's first rank as the swimming center is unquestiond. Prof. Allen has repeatedly proved his ability to make expert swimmers out of old and young who had tho't they could not learn. Many old pupils cordially welcome his return. He is secured to take charge of this club specialty because so many members knew of his remarkable skill and success as the teacher and expert for 5 years with the Florida East Coast Hotels at Palm Beach, and for 8 years with the well known Chicago natatorium.

Bath cabin and balconies

Bathing. Bathing facilities are the best in the mountains, where the waters are usually too cold for comfort. This is due to the club lake front being on a long sloping sand beach where the sun makes the shallow water several degrees warmer. The club has 32 free dressing rooms for lake bathing supplied with Turkish towels. A full supply of suits for young and old is kept for sale and to let. The company sure to be gatherd on the upper and lower balconies of the lakehouse is entertaind mornings and afternoons and often evenings by expert swimming, diving and frolicking in the water, for at no other mountain resort are water sports so popular.

Boating and bathing accidents. The great development of boating and bathing at the club is largely due to the unusual precautions against possible accidents. We keep expert swimmers on duty thruout the season on both sides the narrow lake with fast boats, life preservers, lines and belts in readiness for instant use. During regular bathing hours in addition to the swimming teachers an extra patrol is kept on the water and Prof. Allen has full authority to prevent as well as discourage any undue risks specially on the part of children. Nothing is so attractiv and healthful in the warm months as these water sports. Many families who will not risk accidents elsewhere trust their little people constantly on the club water front under these thoro precautions.

Club carry from Mirror to Placid

Boating. The club is often said to live in or on the water, boating and bathing are such prominent specialties. It has 9 boat houses and the finest fleet in the mountains of over 100 boats, including 20 different patterns, so that each person may find what he most likes in small craft. There are besides the ordinary Adirondack boats found at other resorts, broader and safer boats for families and children, narrower and faster boats for those who like sliding seats, outriggers and spoons, St

Lawrence skiffs, ladies gigs, working boats, the special pattern of club guideboats made in our own shops, sail boats, evening pastimes, canvas and other varieties. There are also 20 birch bark, Canadian, Peterboro and canvas, paddling and sailing canoes. A professional boat builder has his repair shop at the main boat house so that every boat is kept constantly in perfect repair. The club carry connects Placid with Mirror and there are numerous convienent landings on the 3 lakes. There are boats at $3, $4, $5 and $6 a week, according to size and cost. For those owning their own boats there is a charge of $1 a

week for storage, care and cleaning thru the season and of $1 a week lake tax for necessary expenses of maintaining boat houses, landings, life patrol and other boating expenses. By common consent the club is conceded to have unequald facilities for safety and pleasure connected with boating.

Regattas, races and tournaments. Besides the annual Adirondack regatta the last of August, there will be frequent trial races between club houses and crews and a series of tournaments and field days to stimulate interest in golf, tennis, basket ball, roque, swimming and the various other outdoor sports and games for which facilities have been so liberally provided. Members are askt to assist this movement to increase outdoor life by attracting nonparticipants to attend races, match games or tournaments.

Club landing, St Eustace church, Mirror lake

Excursions. Complete camping outfits are lent to those wishing to camp, picnic or climb. Walking, cycling and outdoor parties are encouraged by substantial lunches free to those absent at meal times. The cycle room is not only for storage, but for cleaning and repairs. Every reasonable and practicable effort is made to increase yearly the present high standard of outdoor life and exercise which adds so much to both health and happiness.

Bowling. The club 'Rumble' with 3 alleys is, because of the noise, preferably on the other shore adjoining the west lakehouse, and reacht by the south path round the lake, or by boat in 5 minutes from Clubhouse. Members may reserve alleys for definit hours by registering or telefoning in advance.

Lake and cathedral fires. The lake fires are a specialty of the club. At 6 points where shallow water allowd stone piers 20 ft square have been built up above the surface. Hay rack loads of brush and heavier fuel are piled high on these, and on lake fire nights at 8 p. m. (after September at 7 30) these are lighted. The flames streaming high in air light the lake as if by artificial moonlight and the ever changing lights and shadows fascinate others than fire worshipers.

On a stone foundation, carefully protected, the 'cathedral fire' is similarly built in the forest, 10 minutes from Clubhouse. The trunks of a thousand forest trees on the side toward the great column of flame are brightly lighted while the opposit side is in darkness. The wierd effect is like a vast cathedral at night with one strong electric light at a central point. As the fire dies down it is common to have antifonal songs from the benches scattered among the trees. To hundreds these club fires have been one of the most beautiful sights of their lives.

Float nights. These are also a club specialty. About July 20, August 15 and September 10 there is a general illumination of Clubhouse, the lake front and the fleet of 100 small boats, which go thru various evolutions, after which the 5 lake fires are lighted together and by their light the evening closes with singing in the boats clusterd near the swimming school. The club has over 2000 Chinese and Japanese lanterns for these monthly floats, which produce a wonderfully beautiful effect on the still surface of Mirror lake. First and second prizes are offerd each year to the most artistic, the most effectiv and the most original designs.

Golf. While the club has from the first playd golf, it has recently made it its leading specialty, expending over $20,000 on land and preparation of links, including golf house and library, and teachers and practice courts The general location was fixt by an ex-world's champion, selected as the best living authority. Every hole was laid out under his personal direction and he pronounced the location unexceld in the entire country for magnificence of views, attractiv surroundings and picturesque diversity in the surface The oldest farm in the section was selected because it had a turf impossible to secure in land more recently cleard. The long course is over 3000 yards but tees have been moved up on several holes so that last year it was playd as 2625 yards with holes as follows: Tahawus, 351; Notch, 298; Cobble, 295; Saddleback, 249; Valleyview, 355; Ampersand, 152; Indian pass, 361: Santanoni, 292; St Armand, 274. The short one of 6 holes and 1400 yards is for ladies who do not

Lake Placid Club   Golf house and library

care to play on the longer course and beginners.   2 trout ponds make desirable water-hazards.   The golf house provides lockers, toilet rooms, golf supplies, refreshments and other conveniences. Adjoining is the large golf library with great stone fireplace and glass sides toward the mountains.   This is a favorit reading and writing resort for those not playing and is also used for the weekly 5 o'clock teas, having kitchen, ladies rooms, etc.   Car-

riage roads, cycle paths and trails have been built thru the forest to main highways, lake and Clubhouse, so that the golf houses are most conveniently accessible from all directions. A golf-man is in constant attendance to supervise caddies and houses and look after the comfort of members and a competent teacher is available for those wishing instruction. Many people who have seen scores of links pronounce these the most attractiv they have ever found.

Whitney, Whiteface and Cobble from golf links

The 6 hole course and the privilege of both north and south golf houses are entirely free to club members. This includes golf library, facilities for refreshments and afternoon teas and the right to buy all supplies at New York prices without advance for double expressage charged here. $3000 was spent on the 9 hole course on request of those expressing readiness to pay the following moderate fees to help meet the extra cost.

	Season	Week	Day
1 player.	$10 ..	$2 ..	$ 50
2 in same family.	15 ..	3 ..	1 ..
3 "	17 50	4 ..	1 50
4 "	20 ..	5 ..	2 ..

For each additional player in the same family $2.50 a season or $1 a week is added. The day price is uniformly 50c.

Caddies. To guard against overcharge, dishonesty or incompetence every caddy approved by the golfman wears a badge and number, which is taken from him for incivility or inefficiency. Players pay no money to caddies but buy tickets at the first tee, unless they prefer to caddy for each other or provide their own caddies. This avoids making change and 'tips.' The golfman pays the caddy the money for each ticket turnd in and thus is sure of opportunity to correct any faults reported by players. The cheaper short course ticket is of different color and is good for either the regular 6 hole course or for 6 holes of the long course. Caddy tickets are 25c for long and 15c for short course.

Indoor amusements. Golf, boating, driving, riding and all outdoor sports have receivd unusual attention, but provision has also been made specially for evenings and occasional rainy days and for those who specially enjoy indoor recreations. Photografers have free dark rooms with the best facilities for developing. The music room, seating 300, with stage, curtains, dressing room, etc. provides accommodations for music, dramatics, tableaus, and entertainments for the Village improvement society or the churches, and the new game room will contain facilities for all the best indoor games. There are 4 libraries, nature study, bird and other classes, music, dancing, dramatics, billiards, pool, bowling and all the most desirable indoor games for old and young. Only the more important are mentiond.

Library. The club was founded by authors, librarians and book lovers, who make good books a leading feature. The 4 large library rooms are equipt with library tables, reading chairs and study lamps and are kept quiet. Besides the large libraries in the main house and at Adirondack Lodge there is the lake library over the water, 31x62 feet, two thirds of the sides open in fair weather, all inclosed in glass for storms, with open fires for cold days. The golf library adjoining the golf house is about the same size and has similar provisions.

The library is not a mere collection of books and rooms in which to read them, but a library in the modern broad sense, including the club's whole intellectual life, literature, science, art, history or any lectures or other work undertaken It is not to start a summer school or bore people with efforts to 'improve their minds,' but to provide liberally for those who find in intellectual life their greatest rest and pleasure. To encourage members interested to study club specialties more thoroly in the summer's leisure, collections are being developt of the best books on golf, boating, driving, nature study, birds, mountain climbing, camping, forestry, farming, home economics, health, juvenilia, outdoor and indoor amusements, sports, games and allied subjects.

The club has nearly 2000 books most of them selected as best for club use Besides the latest and best light summer reading, largely fiction, there is ample provision of the most askt for more substantial reading and also 20 leading periodicals, a reference library of the best general and special cyclopedias, atlases, gazetteers, indexes and dictionaries of various subjects including German, French, Italian, Spanish, Latin and Greek, besides the Century, Standard and Webster for English.   It takes 10 of the best newspapers for general use and personal copies can be had at the office.

This large expense is incurred because so many of our members are literary workers and have found it practicable to combine the most efficient work with a delightful vacation, to spend a long summer with their families in the wonderful tonic air of Placid, giving part of every day to outdoor amusements and the rest to the desk Several well-known books have been written at the club and this feature is steadily growing.   Some wish to leave all work behind and play solidly for a few weeks vacation.   Others have learnd that they get more rest and new strength from doubling the length of vacation and working half the time.   By utilizing rainy days and evenings the net result of the summer is much better and the head of the family for the first time feels it practicable to share all the long outing with the rest.   Judges with opinions to write out, lawyers with cases to study, authors with books and articles to prepare, editors with weekly or monthly demands for copy, in fact scores of people, with the libraries, stenografers, typewriters and other facilities provided at the club as at no hotel, are finding it practicable to take a longer vacation than they had before thought possible.

Addresses. The club is not burdend with lecture courses but each season many prominent representatives of the best

thought visit the club and several accept invitations to give
their special message in one of the large rooms. Similarly we
have some of the best pulpit orators in the country who preach
for a single Sunday for one of the 4 flourishing churches on
the opposit shore of the narrow lake, P. E , methodist, baptist
and Roman catholic. The presbyterians hold weekly services
in the baptist church. The last and largest building is St
Eustace which in 1900 had a choral service and vested choir.
In 1901 besides the new church and rector's camp on Placid,
the large number of enthusiastic churchmen who summer at
Placid have, chiefly thru the liberality and devotion of the
rector, Rev. W. W. Moir, lately assistant rector of the Church
of the Holy Communion in New York, furnisht a large rectory
near the Placid library, and have built and equipt a parish
house seldom equald even in the large cities. This has assem-
bly and dressing rooms, offices and kitchen, and all facilities
for meetings and entertainments, a complete gymnasium of the
most modern apparatus, 2 bowling alleys, billiard and pool
tables, shower, needle and other baths, lockers, boat houses,
etc all available to summer visitors as well as to all-the-year
members   2 college graduates specially traind for the work
give their entire time to making this parish house a center for
everything which tends to the improvement of the village.
This remarkable development in the work of St Eustace-by-the-
lakes will increase still more the markt tendency of churchmen
and their families to summer in Placid.

Entertainments. The village and the great hotels across
the lake have very full provision of concerts and other summer
entertainments for those who care to attend. The club council
allows only now and then one of the best which investigation
shows to be worthy the special permission required. The club
is not a public hotel but a great private estate. The entertainments allowd are only those which might be invited to a
large country place to entertain a house party. Morningside
as a private park is wholly free from the annoyances of pedlers,
solicitors and 'entertainers,' which prove such a nuisance in
many summer resorts. All these are excluded unless on special
permission granted only to those whose presence is desirable to
the members.

Music. As those who wish greater quiet can now secure it in the cottages, or in the libraries or parlors which are at the opposit end from the music room, the council has decided on having good music, 3 or 4 pieces, not less than 4 times each week. In addition there will be the 'Sunday night singing' as usual in which all are invited to participate. The grand piano is reservd for concerts and expert pianists where the best instrument in the best condition is demanded. The uprights are for dancing and ordinary use. A music library has been started with a generous supply of both Plymouth and church hymnals and numerous copies of college and popular song collections for the frequent 'sings' in which all are invited to join. Additions are invited from members interested.

There will also be occasional music at Adirondack Lodge, the golf houses and the lake library, in which ⅔ of the sides can be thrown open thus making practically an open air concert for those in boats or on the balconies in the warm evenings.

Amateur music. Accomplisht musicians have always a cordial hearing and there will be recitals and concerts at frequent intervals according to the musical talent at the club, but annoyance to guests from children strumming the pianos or making discordant efforts at amateur music is not allowd.

Even good music is subject to this house rule: 'Musical instruments may be playd in the music rooms, lakehouses, golf-houses and on piazzas, but not in parlors, library, office or private rooms or between 10 p m. and 8 a. m. or during the "quiet hour," 3–5 p. m. The pianos will be closed and all noise that would disturb sleepers stopt promptly at 10 p. m '

Dancing. There will be music, 3 or more pieces, for dancing from 8–10 p. m. in the music room 2 nights each week and a monthly german about July 30, August 15 and September 10. Refreshments will be servd in the tea room or the tower. There will also be music at the hours selected by the council for children's dancing.

Dramatics. The club has unusual provision for dramatics and other entertainments Besides the usual parlors and libraries and 2 lakehouses, it built in 1900 a music room 32 x 80 with 200 ft of piazza 13 ft wide surrounding and opening out of it by glass doors and windows so that many of the audience prefer the piazza seats This room has a raisd stage 18 x 32 with curtain and men's and women's dressing rooms. Immediately over the stage are the tea and refreshment rooms At Adirondack Lodge the theater is a separate building and has stage and dressing rooms, wings and simple scenery There are also at both Clubhouse and Lodge choice spots in the forest for open air dramatics and other entertainments.

Shuffleboard. There are 3 new shuffleboards for 1901.

Photografy. 3 dark rooms at Clubhouse, Westside and Adirondack Lodge with conveniences for developing are free to all. It is expected however that one copy with label and date of any picture of general interest will be contributed to the albums of photografs made by members. No other books will afford more entertainment in future years and it is considerd a compliment to have copies selected for these. As there is no place richer in beautiful subjects for the camera, much attention is given to amateur photografy.

Museum. We wish everything pertaining to the Placid section, not only books, pamflets, clippings, or photografs, but also objects of historic or scientific interest, specimens of flora, fauna, minerals, rocks, in short anything of interest to those who love our beautiful natural surroundings. While we prefer specimens labeld and mounted, everything worth keeping will be properly cared for. As interest and cooperation warrant there will be develop an arboretum with specimen trees labeld with scientific and popular names, a botanic garden for wild flowers and plants, a zoo of living animals, an aquarium of nativ fish, and a collection of mounted specimens of our nativ birds and animals. The library has the best illustrated books on all these subjects. The state scientific officers have greatly helpt these new features by recognizing the peculiar advantages of this township for lovers of nature who wish to study it at its best. Experts have prepared bulletins with maps and illustrations on the geology, flora and fauna. All 3 can be had at the office. During each season as interest justifies there will be lectures or familiar illustrated talks for those wishing to cultivate their outdoor tastes and know more of nature in its varied forms in the Placid region.

Members interested in our plans for museum zoo. botanic garden, ... uested to send . . . . ing to cooperate. We have now provided rooms and needed facilities, garden space and necessary help, and these features will be developt as fast as members do their part.

Gifts. Members interested respond generously to the standing request for gifts to this library and museum supplementing the liberal annual expenditures from club funds. Being so far from large libraries we gladly include in the permanent club collection any books, pamflets or other additions which one might want during a long summer. Each member should look over his shelves and book table on starting for the club and bring what he is willing to spare to help in the present activ effort to enlarge our club collections The giver's name will be enterd on the bookplate except in cases of cheap editions or unimportant books, which are kept on the shelves, tho not counted as really a part of the library. Gifts of these books, which are often not wanted at home, are requested, as almost everything unobjectionable in character is sooner or later wanted Duplicates can be given away to advantage in our own or other Adirondack villages, so that everything can be used.

Kindergarten. Traind kindergartners take the little ones 5 mornings a week for nature study, games and the many helps to development given better by this method than any other. This is equally valuable to the children and to the mothers who are thus relievd of all care thru the mornings.

Tutors. Provision is made yearly for competent instructors for those who from illness or other cause have more or less school or college work to make up before fall. In this way the needed work is done better and more cheaply and the family is kept together. It is a delight to a healthy boy, whose heart is broken at leaving all the club recreations behind, to learn that he can do the necessary work in 2 or 3 hours a day and have the rest of his time for unalloyd happiness. It is very desirable that those wishing instruction of any kind should send early word to the superintendent.

Bird lessons. Birds are to both young and old a fascinating outdoor subject. Midsummer visitors forget that in moulting season birds are quiet and little observd by those untraind, but several recognized authorities on birds who have visited the club report our woods unusually rich in bird life. For 1901

we have secured Miss Mary Mann Miller, whose training at
the New Jersey state normal school and at Smith college and
Cornell university, with years of experience as a teacher of
bird lessons, has qualified her admirably for this work   She
has also been intimately associated with her mother, Mrs Olive
Thorne Miller, whose many books on birds are so widely read.
Miss Miller will be in residence at the club all of June and July,
the best months for bird classes.

There will be separate courses for adults and for children,
each of 10 classes and 10 field lessons.   Different classes will
be formd from June 1 to August 1, at prices from $5 to $10 a
course, according to number working together.

The classes are pland for those who know nothing of the
subject, being untechnical in treatment, tho strictly correct as
to facts.   The pupil is carefully instructed in the use of the
manual and in methods of field observation, and has practical
work in each under the teacher's eye.

The student is introduced to the common birds, told something of their habits of life and peculiarities of manner and
markings, which will make identification easy.   Mounted birds,
skins and pictures will be used so pupils may not only become
familiar with the common birds but with the aid of the manual
may readily identify those more rare.   In the field lessons each
has an opportunity to put into practice what has been learnd
and to become familiar with the songs.

The club has bought about 20 of the best books on birds
with the purpose of making this a specialty in its library.   It
has also numerous telescopes and opera glasses to lend to those
who are satisfied to hunt the birds in this way, the use of the
gun being absolutely forbidden on the club estate.   It is desirable that those wishing to join the classes should send word of
the time of their probable arrival at the club.

The following extracts from letters receivd are in answer
to our inquiry of former pupils or those who had special knowledge of Miss Miller's qualifications for the club bird classes.

Miss Mary Mann Miller's efforts to interest people in the
bird life about them, to add another charm to country life and
the summer vacation, are worthy of all encouragement.   She
is likely to prove to any city skeptic that there are at least as
many delightful and profitable acquaintances in the tree tops
and among the meadow grasses about the summer hotels as in
the rocking chairs on its piazzas   *Neltje Blanchan*

Her class of pupils and teachers from our school were
enthusiastic as to the lessons and pursued the course with sus-
tained interest to the end. *Abby B. Morgan, Dearborn Morgan
school, Orange N J*

I am glad to tell you of the pleasure and benefit Miss Miller
brought into our lives.   I think she began teaching in Ludlow

mainly to give new interest in life to an invalid who could watch the birds only from her window. When it was known that Miss Miller was organizing a class, pupils from within a radius of 4 miles asked to be admitted. At the close of the first season we were so enthusiastic that we asked her to return the next spring. It is no easy task to open eyes that see not and ears that hear not; and that is what Miss Miller does. The first season I grew so confused by the many bird songs and notes that I felt my ears were hopeless; but the next spring when I came back I was amazed to find the confusion all gone. It was as if I had new ears, and I felt it was largely due to Miss Miller's perseverance and patience in answering again and again the question, 'What bird is that?' Her pupils here hold her in affection and grateful remembrance, and I personally am happy to number her among my friends. *Mary E. Fletcher*

Miss Miller's wide knowledge of birds is freely imparted, and her love of nature contagious. She left our bird class wildly enthusiastic. We found her everything that could be desired of a teacher. *Abbie L. Baldwin, Ludlow Vt.*

It gives me pleasure to say a word for Miss Miller and her work among the people of Ludlow, Vt. For two seasons I was a member of her class for the study of birds, and I have since derived much pleasure from the pursuit of studies begun under her helpful guidance. As a result of her work I noticed a change in the relations between the birds and the pupils of the school. *Frank L. Bugbee, Prin. Black River Academy, Ludlow Vt.*

Golf links looking south   Mt Jo, Adirondack Lodge, in middle foreground

How to reduce living expenses at the club

The trustees recognize that many of the choicest people wanted as members must consider carefully the cost. Accommodations have therefore been provided at so wide a range of price (50c to $5 a day) as to meet such needs. Those paying high prices for the largest rooms with various extras make it possible to offer smaller rooms with all necessities for health and comfort at a price far less than their proportionate share of the general expense account. The club believes it sound economy thus to tax luxuries rather than necessities. Those who fear cost may be too great should note these points:

1 Use N. Y. C. R R milage, now good from New York, Boston, Buffalo and all intermediate points to Saranac Lake. This reduces one third the fare from Utica up and the club buys any unused coupons at cost. Simply buy enough 500-mile tickets at $10 each. From Boston only 1000-mile tickets are good

2 Send to the club for the half price tickets from Saranac to Placid. Keep all baggage checks for club driver and go up in club carriages, which are quickest and best

3 **Meals.** Prices are invariable, but cost may be reduced to any point wisht by partial or complete housekeeping All needed supplies can be gotten cookt or uncookt from the club or from excellent village markets which deliver free at the door. Housekeeping is as easy and inexpensiv as anywhere. Some have continental breakfast in their cottages or get their own supper and go to the club for dinner at 75c. Other meals are 50c Full board is $1 50; children under 12 and servants in side hall $1 a day. Either plan can be tried and changed if not liked, members having entire freedom to use all the resources of the club, getting any supplies from its kitchen, coolers, storerooms, bakery, farms, garden, etc. or buying elsewhere.

4 **Rooms.** Lower priced rooms may be chosen, as they range from 50c to $5 a day. By going farther from Clubhouse, larger, better and more quiet rooms may be had at a given price. 2 or more may occupy 1 room, as there is no extra charge except $1 a week for extra beds. Tents are more

healthful and give great satisfaction and more space at given cost.

5 Before July 10 and after September 10, rooms, baths and boats are only half price, thus greatly reducing the summer's expenses. The early and late season has more attractions, there is better choice of rooms and many more privileges and economies are possible than when the club is crowded. It is fixt policy to attract early and late guests by making expenses much less in various ways. See "Early and late" circular. Those spending a long season, after paying for 10 weeks are charged only for care of rooms, rent being free for the rest of the season. Season leases can also be made for horses

6 **Amusements.** The amount spent on horses, boats, etc. may be limited as closely as wisht. Many have no bills for these extras. So much is entirely free at the club that incidental expenses are much less than at hotels. Fees or tips are not only not expected but are absolutely prohibited. Many who think club life beyond their means find otherwise on trial. Others much prefer a shorter vacation, if necessary, with all club privileges to a longer time in a less desirable place More than one family have reported that since coming to the club their medical bills have been reduced during the summer and following winter much more than the extra amount expended, because the club protects as fully as possible against the many dangers that menace most summer resorts.

There is at the club absolutely no caste of wealth or social standing based on expenditures. The most popular members are often those who must economize closely. We have yet to learn of the slightest embarrassment in so doing. A hotel caters specially to wealthy guests because from them and their liberal fees, tips and extra patronage of all kinds it makes its chief revenue. The club has no interest in this but seeks to have on the grounds people who enjoy its very different standards and life and who are agreeable summer companions for the other members. This elimination of the money element is a great charm of the club. Those who hesitate on the score of expense should try one season and study the totals as compared with expenses in less desirable places

What adds to cost of rooms

One who reads our cooperativ plans for largely reducing expenses often expects prices of rooms to be lower He forgets perhaps that many expenses run for 12 months and must be met by the receipts of the short midseason of only 2 months, as before and after that, when rooms and boats are half price, only current expenses can be met. Insurance, taxes, repairs and the care of 116 different roofs during the severe storms of winter are just as costly as if all were occupied. The many-fold increase since the club started in 1895, in comforts and attractions free to members is due to the larger number among which fixt charges are divided, to the new facilities for doing all our own work and to other economies which careful organization and study have made possible. While new and larger rooms with private baths and more costly furniture have been added at higher prices, the rent of rooms with which the club started in '95 has not been raisd, the changes having made the average price lower. When the unequald facilities offerd are considerd this is a gratifying record. Some of the reasons why rooms must of necessity cost more at the club than at a hotel are noted below.

1 The cost of administration, repairs and care is much heavier than in a single large building. Nearly every cottage has its parlor with open fire and one or more bath rooms with separate hot water heaters requiring the service of a man twice a day, while coal is $7 50 a ton. In scatterd cottages chambermaids can care for only two thirds as many rooms, thus adding one half to cost of this item

2 Most summer resorts have little land to pay for and care for Our estate of 4000 acres with manifold attractions open free to club members requires keeping miles of roads and walks in repair and other expenses in addition to taxes and interest on a very large investment.

3 Club members are free from the annoyance of the vicious but omnipresent fee and tip system. All employees are engaged with the distinct understanding that no fees are permitted. The club pays higher wages and gives better homes and various extra privileges instead of allowing its guests to supplement insufficient wages with gratuities By its system

the club secures a higher grade of girls who would not accept
positions in ordinary hotels where they must humiliate themselves to 'fish for tips '

4 Many things charged as extras in hotels are free, e. g.
baths are 25c or 50c in most places, while there are 4 free bathrooms in Clubhouse and 1 in each cottage having plumbing.
30 bath cabins with Turkish towels are also free for lake
bathing, which is very popular.

5 There is no charge for luncheons put up for picnic,
excursion and camping parties, or for early or late breakfasts
or teas.

6 Many things are supplied which add greatly to convenience but bring no return, e. g. telefones connecting village
and cottages with club office; docks in various places on both
lakes, for golf links, churches and carries, with convenient
transportation for boats from one lake to the other; 4 libraries
of nearly 2000 choice volumes, with reference books, 20 leading periodicals and papers; free use of village library of about
2000 volumes for which other summer guests are charged a
fee; short golf course; 14 tennis and other courts for outdoor
games; flowers; dark rooms for photografers.

7 The table is supplied with the best obtainable food.
Many hotels put into cold storage eggs, chickens, fruits, vegetables, etc. when they are cheapest and months later serve to
guests when prices are high. The club lays great stress on
having, and incurs large extra expense to secure, the freshest
of eggs, milk and cream, dry pickt poultry, and only such fish,
fruits and vegetables as can be had strictly fresh. The epi-
demics of summer complaint so common in many resorts have
never been known at the club.

These and many other things are done to carry out an
ideal when a different course would be taken if the object were
as in hotels merely to make money. No charge is made for
these various comforts, conveniences and extras except that
included in price of bedrooms The table, livery, laundry and
amusement prices cover only actual cost, only their own proper
expenses being charged to them. Therefore the rooms are the
only source of income from which to meet the heavy general
expenses of the great estate. One who studies its extent and
the necessary cost of its proper maintenance will not feel that

he is charged more than his pro rata share in what might seem
at first a high price for his room. Of rent paid more than one
fifth is used for things which are free to all. Members who
occupy houses not ownd by the club may therefore pay one
fifth what the club would charge for rent and thus become
entitled to all privileges the same as if they occupied club
cottages or rooms and in the rent paid bore their pro rata share
of what is spent for the common use.

Annual dues of members and associates

*This statement is sent to all members and associates each May 1 or on taking rooms
for the season The dues should be sent to the treasurer Asa O Gallup, 15 W 43 st, New
York, and he will return the club receipt entitling to reserve rooms and all privileges
for the calendar year.*

The table, laundry, livery, golf, boating and other amusements are carried on by cooperation, all payments by members
being devoted wholly to necessary expenses of each department. Rent of houses and rooms goes entirely to the estate
and its maintenance and improvement including insurance and
taxes. Libraries, periodicals, music, monthly germans and
float nights, telefones, bath cabins, lawn parties, tennis and
other courts and various other conveniences and amusements
free to all are paid by the annual dues.

Under club rules, the annual dues of $10 are payable each
May 1, unless previously paid for that calendar year on engaging rooms No rooms can be reservd on the club books without
this payment for the year. The heavy initial expenses of each
season are incurred in May before there are any receipts from
the year's business, and it is important that all dues be paid
promptly in order that buildings, grounds and supplies may be
ready on June 1 for the first arrivals.

As the sum thus paid is used as a contingent fund to meet
expenses which benefit all but are not otherwise provided for,
the amount being made small so that it should not be a burden
to any one, it was decided that all members and associates,
except honorary and life members, whether expecting to be at
the club that season or not, should make this payment each
May 1, no one being exempt because of possible absence.

The e dues are to entitle one to engage rooms and to have
meals, etc. at cost. Only one fee is charged a family including

Lake Placid Club   Lakeside dining rooms, lakehouse and library from southwest

498

guests. Those paying their own bills but coming as visitors for less than 2 weeks, are also exempted

At Adirondack Lodge, the forest branch of the club, those who do not pay dues are charged $2 a day for meals, and 50c of this is used for the same purposes as the $10. For one person spending less than 20 days it would be less expensiv to pay the regular rate of $2.

As the dues are a necessary part of the club plan, they can no more be remitted than could the charge for laundry

As there are no other charges or liabilities of any kind except as each member pays his living expenses while at the club, all should be willing to contribute these unusually small annual club dues as a nucleus for extra club expenses. Under this plan, successfully administerd, our members have at their disposal what is now recognized as much the most attractiv summer plant in the Adirondacks.

Hay fever exemption at Lake Placid Club

The following from a letter of a well-known victim of the disease represents fairly the remarkably successful record of the club Physicians know that cases vary greatly, but in no other place is relief so markt for nearly all sufferers. By believing the advertisements so common of 'no hay fever,' many victims of the disease have seriously aggravated their difficulty by a stay where there was little or no relief 15 years of experiments and correspondence to find the safest refuge in the United States resulted in selecting Morningside as the location for the club

I am often askt regarding the claims of Lake Placid as a refuge from hay fever by those who know how aggravated is my own case and how persistently I have sought relief in many parts of this country and abroad. My experience with hay cold is wide enough to know that it, is impossible to predict absolutely the effect on any patient from the experience of others, but for the 8th year I find Placid giving more relief than any other place I have ever been, the next best being Mackinaw island in Lake Superior. My own experience has been repeated by many others Some hay cold victims have suffered seriously at Placid on the village side of the lake, where during the season fine dust from the road is constantly flying Usually prompt relief is secured by crossing to Morningside, east of the lake, and thus escaping the dust The Lake Placid club chose its location with special reference to this exemption, its 3 principal promoters all being sufferers from the dreaded disease. Results have fully confirmd the wisdom of that choice

10 years ago I was free except for 6 weeks beginning August 19, but neglect to spend enough time in an exempt locality resulted in bringing on the disease earlier and earlier till I am now forced to live during July, August and September at Placid, where I am as comfortable as any one else if I avoid driving on dusty roads. Like most victims, I am only too glad if my long search for a reliable asylum can save others from suffering not only during the hay cold season, but also in many cases more or less thru the year as a result of failure to find exemption in midsummer and fall.

Lake Placid Club · Lakeside · lake house and library from Forest · 453

Club printed matter

The club willingly sends information to those interested. To avoid mistakes use the initials below, which indicate each publication definitly.

O Briefest outline of objects and methods.
C Descriptiv circular with half tones.
AL Circular of forest branch. Adirondack Lodge.
Cm Members, associates and guests; eligibility.
Pp Selected half tones of club and surroundings, postal size.
Pn Half tones, note size, 12.5x20 cm.
Pm Maps of Morningside and vicinity.
F Floor plans and complete price lists.
Q Distinctiv features of the club.
A Amusements and recreations and cost.
Hf On immunity from hay fever.
R Annual report and announcement to members of plans for season.
Ub Bonds and capital stock of club plant.
V Village improvement society year book on Lake Placid as a summer home.
H Fully illustrated, indext handbook, all above (151p.) bound together.

A lakeside camp

INDEX

In paging Report for 1901, space was left in Handbook for circular on Amusements. This proved too long and was put after Report, p. 109-40 being therefore omitted.